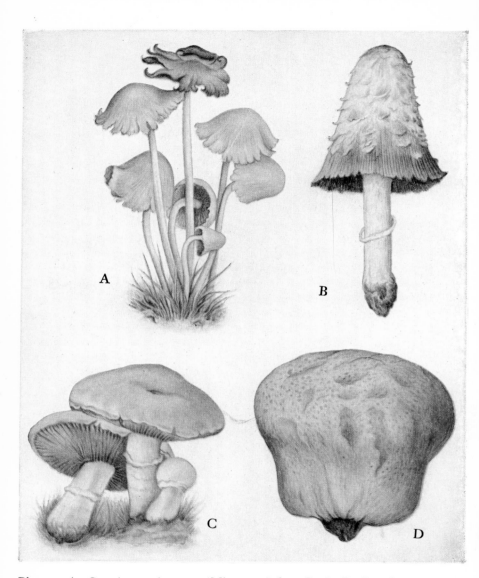

Plate 1. A. *Coprinus micaceus* (Mica, or Inky, Cap). B. *Coprinus comatus* (Shaggymane). C. *Agaricus campestris* (Field Mushroom). D. *Calvatia caelata* (Carved Puffball). All edible.

COMMON
Edible Mushrooms

by

Clyde M. Christensen
Professor of Plant Pathology
University of Minnesota

THE UNIVERSITY OF MINNESOTA PRESS
Minneapolis

Printed at Lund Press, Minneapolis

SIXTH PRINTING 1972

ISBN: 0-8166-0509-2

Table of Contents

Mushrooms without Gills

Mushroom Cookery

List of Illustrations

COMMON EDIBLE MUSHROOMS

Common Edible Mushrooms

About Mushrooms

Mushrooms have long been regarded all over the world as the most delectable and succulent of foods. Their peculiarly delicate flavor charmed the luxury-loving Roman aristocrats more than twenty centuries ago, as it charms all civilized folk today. But most of us do not realize that the mushrooms we buy at the grocery store, either fresh or in cans, represent only one of the many edible kinds and that countless others make equally delightful eating. For edible mushrooms are to be found everywhere — in front yards, on shade trees, in parks, fields, and forests.

All too often these evanescent plants are looked upon as strange, unearthly things, to be feared and avoided, if not trodden upon and destroyed. Yet many of these same mushrooms that spring up in such prodigal abundance are both savory and delicious, eagerly sought by the epicure but to be had by anyone for the mere fun of hunting and picking them. To those who do not know them the best are made to share the reputation of the worst, and all are grouped together under the darkly suggestive name of *toadstools*, malevolent things that smack of night and thunder and pouring rain, fit company for goblins and witches!

There is a rather general feeling that only an expert can tell an edible mushroom from a poisonous one, and that he can do it only by some obscure and secret test. For this reason people who would enjoy eating wild mushrooms shun the many good ones for fear of confusing them with the few bad kinds, though anyone can easily learn to know the common edible mushrooms well enough to pick and eat them with perfect safety. Some of them, in fact, are even easier to recognize than flowers or trees, and we need go

Note: Assistance in the preparation of the colored plates and of Diagrams 1 and 2 in this book was provided by the personnel of Work Projects Administration, Official Project No. 165–1–71–124, sponsored by the University of Minnesota.

3

no farther for them than the front lawn, or a neighboring park or woodlot. With no more time or trouble than it takes to learn to recognize half a dozen different kinds of flowers or shrubs that grow in our gardens we can learn to know an equal number of the choicer mushrooms.

There are about half a dozen types of mushrooms that appear regularly in sufficient abundance to make it worth while getting acquainted with them from the culinary standpoint. No special abilities, training, or equipment are necessary, and the time and effort expended will be amply rewarded with many a dish of fungi fresh from the field.

There is no risk in eating wild mushrooms of proved quality, kinds that have been eaten in many lands and for thousands of years. There *is* danger in eating all wild mushrooms indiscriminately. Even children who go berry picking in the woods do not pick and eat all kinds of berries, because they have been taught that some are good and others are inedible or harmful. Instead, they go after certain specific, *known* kinds. In the same way one should not pick and eat any wild mushrooms he happens to find but should seek morels, shaggymanes, puffballs, or other particular kinds, like those described in this book, that can be recognized with ease and certainty and that are positively known to be good. If you follow this rule you will find them as delicious, wholesome, and safe as any other wild vegetable, though less nourishing than most. To those who know and like them, their flavor more than makes up for their lack of nourishment. Indeed, their low calory value recommends them to many!

This book has been written to introduce a number of the common edible mushrooms so that people without previous training or experience can learn how to recognize them, where and when to find them, and how to prepare them for eating. Since it is intended for the beginner it will *not* enable you to identify offhand any mushroom you happen to pick up. Of the hundreds of common species only about fifty are described, and these fifty were chosen primarily on the basis of ease of recognition and common occurrence throughout the country. Three general groups and one single kind have been selected from the fifty and included in a special section called "The Foolproof Four." These are considered to be four of the most easily and surely recognized, most abundant and widespread, and most desirable in flavor and texture of all our common edible mushrooms. Any discerning person should be able to gather and eat these as safely as he gathers and eats blueberries or wild strawberries.

Emphasis throughout the book is placed upon the obviously sound idea that you must learn to know those that are absolutely safe and good, and avoid all others. This constant emphasis is not meant to convey the impression that eating wild mushrooms is more dangerous than eating other wild plants, or that there are more kinds of poisonous mushrooms than there are of equally poisonous other plants, because there definitely are not. It is merely that most of us have had some training and experience in distinguishing the higher plants, and we look upon them not as plants in general but as specific kinds, such as blueberries, poison ivy, and so on. So that you may learn in the same way to know the specific kinds of mushrooms that are most harmful to man, a few of the very poisonous species are also described in this book, as well as several poisonous species that are closely related to, and sometimes confused with, certain edible ones.

It must be repeated, however, that these are not the *only* poisonous mushrooms; they are merely the most common and most deadly. Excessive caution is always necessary even if you are a trained mycologist. Therefore remember: IF YOU FIND A MUSHROOM THAT IS *not* DESCRIBED AS *edible* IN THIS BOOK, *don't eat it!*

Your attention is respectfully called to the last section of the book, to which a number of people experienced in the art of mushroom cookery have contributed recipes. Some of these recipes are new and original; one at least is more than three hundred years old. A few are designed to bring out the best qualities of specific kinds of mushrooms; others can be applied to a large variety.

5

Those who wish to delve deeper into the field of fungi will find the books about mushrooms and mushroom cultivation listed on pages 119–20 of great value.

How and Where They Grow

To those only casually acquainted with it, the entire fungus world is strange and unnatural. Seemingly nourished only by rain, mushrooms spring up in abundance in the night and are gone by noon. Indeed, some of the more delicate kinds are found only in the brief period between dawn and sunrise; before the dew has dried they have withered and disappeared, unsuspected and unseen by many a slug-a-bed. They seem to be at the mercy of their environment, and one wonders how they persist and multiply.

The explanation is simple. The mushroom we see is only a small part of the fungus as a whole. The growing, or vegetative, part, by means of which the fungus gets its food and endures from year to year, is hidden in the ground. This spawn, or *mycelium*, is made up of a multitude of growing cells. The mildew you have seen on bread, the mold on jelly or preserves, the cottony growth that permeates the litter of the forest floor are all mycelium. It continues to grow from year to year, lying dormant in winter and in dry periods but becoming active almost at once when conditions are again favorable. It is from this actively growing mycelium, whose span of life is measured in years, decades, or even centuries, that the mushroom arises for its brief appearance.

Evidence of the longevity of this mycelium is found in rotting trees, where the mycelium that causes the decay may live for centuries, advancing slowly year by year until finally the tree is so weakened that it topples over. Further evidence is found in fairy rings, those remarkable circles of mushrooms that once were thought to mark the path of dancing fairies. These rings are formed in this way: A few spores of one of the fairy-ring mush-

6

rooms fall upon a favorable place and begin to grow. If the soil is fairly uniform, an approximately circular patch of mycelium develops. After a few years mushrooms spring up near the outer border of this circle. Each year the mycelium advances regularly outward, and mushrooms again arise at its outer edge, thus forming an ever-growing fairy ring. Lack of uniformity in the soil or accidents of one kind or another may interrupt the regular outward growth of mycelium during the passage of years, so that few large complete circles are formed, although people have found some that were more than fifty feet across. By measuring the rate of advance over a period of years botanists have calculated that some of these fairy rings are almost four centuries old. Thus these fragile and transitory fruit bodies that are born, mature, and die in the shortness of a day spring from roots that may outlive many generations of men.

Mushrooms reproduce chiefly by means of spores. The mushroom as we know it is merely the fruit body of the plant; its function is to produce the largest number of spores in the shortest possible time and liberate them into the air. These spores are similar to the seeds of higher plants, but they differ from seeds in the simplicity of their structure and in their very small size. A typical mushroom spore is a single, thin-walled cell about 1/2,500 of an inch long, so small and light that it can be wafted about by the slightest breeze.

When a spore alights on the ground where moisture and food are available, it absorbs water, swells, and forms a protuberance on one side; this grows into a long filament, or *hypha*. The hypha may live for a short time on the food stored in the spore, but the spore is so small that this reserve food is not sufficient for more than mere inception of growth. The filament continues to grow and eventually forms a dense network of branched mycelium.

Many species of mushrooms form slowly just beneath the surface of the soil, developing over a period of weeks or even months. When they are almost completely formed, if there is enough moisture present, the stem elongates rather suddenly and

7

raises the cap up into the air, the cap expanding as it is raised. Evidence that mushrooms have been formed below the surface of the ground can be seen in the pieces of dirt and debris that cling to the tops of freshly expanded specimens. These soft and delicate mushrooms can exert a surprising force when expanding in this way; they sometimes raise up rocks of several pounds' weight and have been known to force paving blocks up out of the street.

Young mushrooms of some species are entirely enclosed in a protecting sheath of mycelium, which is broken as the mushroom expands. If this sheath remains as a cup-like structure around the base of the stem it is called a cup or *volva*. The patches or warts of mycelium scattered over the caps of some species of Amanita are the remains of this enclosing sheath. In many species a veil is formed by another sheath of mycelium extending from the edge of the cap to the stem, just beneath the gills. If this breaks at the margin of the cap when the cap expands, it may remain on the stem as a ring. If it breaks at the stem, remnants of it may hang from the margin of the cap for a short time, until they wither and disappear. Many species, however, lack cup or ring, or both.

The spores of mushrooms and of the molds related to them are among the most persistent and numerous of our uninvited guests. Borne by the wind, they literally fill the air we breathe, fall unseen upon the food we eat, and even settle into our morning coffee as we drink it. Unnoticed and usually harmless, they are nevertheless omnipresent. When mushroom spores land in a favorable spot, they germinate, produce mycelium, and eventually give rise to another crop of mushrooms and spores. Since most mushrooms live on decaying vegetable matter they are likely to be abundant on various kinds of plant debris. Grassy places and forests are favorite environments. A few have very special tastes and grow only on the dung of certain kinds of animals, on specific kinds of trees, on the cones of certain evergreens, around the roots of certain grasses, on the caps of certain other mushrooms, and even on so unnourishing a thing as plaster!

Most of the edible kinds have their favorite environments, although these are not likely to be so sharply restricted as those just mentioned. By knowing where to look for them we can save much aimless wandering. The elm Pleurotus, for example, inhabits the heartwood of elms and box elder trees especially and puts out its fat fruit bodies at knotholes or branch stubs ten or twenty feet above the ground. The oyster mushroom, closely related to the elm Pleurotus, prefers newly cut logs and stumps, and fruits so regularly and abundantly on them that in Germany people have practiced watering new stumps to induce the production of this fungus. Nearly all fairy-ring mushrooms and puffballs prefer grassy fields and pastures, where the soil has not been disturbed too much; the shaggymanes like roadsides; and morels grow best in wooded areas.

In general, then, if one is hunting mushrooms to eat, he must look for them in grassy meadows and pastures, on compost heaps, on and near stumps and fallen trees, and even within hollow logs, on the ground in shady forests, on branch stubs of living trees, and all up and down the trunks and limbs of dead trees.

Mushrooms Edible and Poisonous

There are a number of ways by which some people claim to be able to distinguish edible mushrooms from poisonous ones — tests such as the blackening of a silver fork or of a silver coin placed in the pot where the fungi are cooking, or involving such easily visible characters as the color of the cap or the gills or the presence of a cup at the base of the stem, or the even more subtle characters of odor, texture, or season of appearance. Each will swear by his own particular test and will submit as evidence of its efficacy his own health and well-being after he has picked and eaten wild mushrooms for years. This is obvious proof that the mushrooms he ate were edible; it does not prove that those he avoided or discarded were not just as good as those he ate. Such tests will seem to be authentic if poisonous species are so uncom-

9

mon as to be rarely or never found, but many a mushroom convicted as poisonous by any of these tests might well have been edible and delicious. In fact, it can be stated flatly that no one of these tests, nor all of them put together, will serve to separate the poisonous kinds from the edible.

For the proof of the mushroom is in the eating. Some kinds are known to be edible because people have eaten them without ill effects, and others are known to be poisonous because when eaten they have caused illness. In this respect mushrooms do not differ from other poisonous plants, such as water hemlock and deadly nightshade. There is no external sign by which we can *see* that water hemlock is fatal if eaten, and we know that it is only because people in the past have been poisoned by it and their survivors have described the plant accurately enough so that others might recognize and avoid it. One of our most generally grown and delicious of garden vegetables, the tomato, was not commonly grown in England or America for more than two hundred years after it had been taken to Europe from South America. Because of its resemblance to its near relative, the deadly nightshade, it was considered poisonous and was cultivated only as a botanical curiosity. Only by eating it did people find out that it was not poisonous. The same thing is true of mushrooms. Of two that are closely related one may be poisonous and the other perfectly wholesome, and only by knowing the distinguishing characters of each can one separate the good from the bad.

An example will illustrate how subtle this difference sometimes is. *Lepiota morgani* is a poisonous mushroom and if eaten causes severe, though seldom fatal, illness. *Lepiota rachodes* is edible and delicious. These two are so closely related and look so much alike that even an expert can tell them apart only by the fact that mature specimens of *L. morgani*, the poisonous one, have green gills and deposit pale green spores, whereas the spores and gills of *L. rachodes*, the edible one, are white. Half-grown specimens of the two kinds are identical. *L. morgani* commonly comes up in the spring, *L. rachodes* in the fall, and people who know them only slightly are likely to assume that a specimen found in the fall is *L. rachodes* and eat it forthwith. Usually they are right, but sometimes both species come up together in the fall, and then people who depend upon season of appearance instead of spore color to distinguish them may suffer seriously for their carelessness.

A far more puzzling case is that of the saddle fungus. Throughout Europe many species of wild mushrooms are collected and sold in the public markets. To avoid the danger of confusing the edible with the poisonous kinds, only those deemed safe are permitted to be sold, the markets being inspected to enforce the regulations. *Gyromitra esculenta*, the common brown saddle fungus, is considered one of the choice edible spring mushrooms both in Europe and America, and for many years great quantities of it have been gathered and sold in the public markets of France and Germany. Within the last decade, however, its sale has been banned in a number of cities because it was proved beyond all doubt to have occasioned several deaths from poisoning.

Some say that there are two varieties of *Gyromitra esculenta*, one poisonous, the other edible; others say that all individuals of this species contain a toxic, water-soluble acid that leaches out into the water in which the mushrooms are cooked, and that if this water is poured off the mushrooms are good to eat. Still others believe the fungus to be poisonous only when eaten by sick or undernourished people, especially children, or if eaten in excessive quantities. All who have had a wide experience with it admit that under some circumstances it can cause illness and death, yet it continues to be sold in many European cities and certainly is eaten in quantity in both Europe and America. It also continues to poison a few people each year, and not many years ago it is believed to have caused the death of several members of a family in northern Minnesota, all of whom were, by the way, sick and undernourished.

How, then, is one to be certain that any specific mushroom is edible? The only way is to learn to recognize with absolute certainty all the specimens gathered for eating, and to look up their edibility in a standard text. *Never eat those about whose identity there is even the slightest doubt.*

How to Identify Them

Many kinds of edible fungi like morels, shaggymanes, inky caps, puffballs, the sulphur shelf fungus, the cone fungus, the Jew's ear, and a host of others can be recognized by the general shape, size, and color alone. Once you have studied the actual specimens, or even good pictures of them, you can recognize them anywhere. For this reason you should become familiar with the pictures and descriptions in this book *before* you go fungus hunting.

To identify some species of gill fungi, however, you need to know whether there is a sheath or cup around the base of the stem, or a veil extending from the stem to the edge of the half-expanded cap, as it does in the cultivated kinds you buy in the store. You must observe whether the gills come up close to the stem but do not touch it or are attached to it or run a short way down the stem. In many cases this means that to be sure of your fungus you need not only a single specimen but several, in various stages of development. (See Diagram 1.) The characters that distinguish certain kinds are present at only one stage of growth and unless you find specimens in this stage you cannot be certain of their identity. For this reason even experienced amateur and professional mycologists find many single mushrooms about whose identity they are in doubt. If they are gathering fungi to eat and not to study, they leave these doubtful ones in the woods. You will find many mushrooms that are not described in this book, but unless you know them well, leave them alone! *Never eat a fungus that you do not know with absolute certainty.*

Spore color is one of the simplest aids in the identification of mushrooms with gills. To determine the color of the spores it is necessary to make a spore print (Diagram 2), though deposits of spores are sometimes found on the leaves or grass beneath the

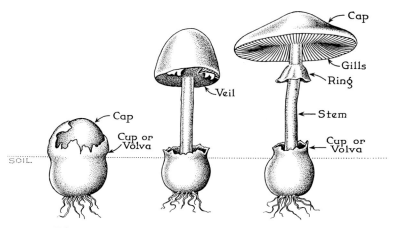

Diagram 1. Three stages in the development of a
typical mushroom.

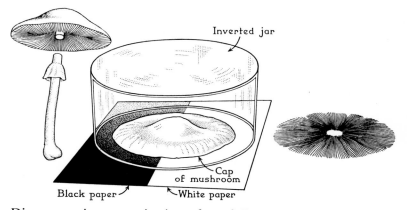

Diagram 2. A spore print is made as follows: The stem is cut off
just below the cap (left); the cap is placed on paper, gills down
(center); the resulting spore print is shown on the right.

13

mushroom cap, and when several are growing close together in a clump the upper ones often make good spore deposits on the caps or stems of the lower. Look for these spore deposits when you pick the mushrooms; they often save time in identifying the fungus.

A spore print is made (see diagram) by cutting off the stem of a mushroom just beneath the cap and placing the cap, gills down, on a piece of paper, covering it with an inverted glass or any other vessel that will keep the air moist and quiet around the cap. It is best to cut the cap into two pieces and place one on black paper and one on white, or to place both black and white paper under the cap. If the cap is dry it must be moistened with water, and in any case it is a good practice to place a piece of wet cotton or paper inside the vessel to keep the cap from drying out while the spores are being deposited.

In an hour or two enough spores usually will have fallen from the gills to make a visible print. The color of the spores often differs from the color of the gills; hence the color of the latter is not a reliable guide. Anyone just beginning to become acquainted with some of the common edible mushrooms will find such spore prints a most valuable aid in identification, and well worth the bother involved in making them. The gilled mushrooms are divided arbitrarily into five groups according to the color of their spores. These colors are white, yellow to yellow-brown, pink, purple to purple-brown, and black. Representatives of all five groups are taken up in this book, in that order. Mushrooms without gills are discussed under the common names of the groups with which they are associated.

Gathering Them

Before starting on your mushroom hunt you should study the pictures and descriptions of at least a number of the common groups and individual kinds described in the book thoroughly enough to know the characters by which they are recognized.

Those starting from scratch might do well to restrict themselves to "The Foolproof Four" for a time. As knowledge is gained and confidence increases, go on to those in which spore color is a necessary identifying character. Since all the characters other than spore color can be determined readily in the field, compare your specimens with the pictures and descriptions in the book as you find them, leaving only spore color to be determined at home. The pictures do not show comparative sizes, but the range in size of each kind is given in the text.

When you set out on a mushroom-hunting expedition you need no equipment other than a clean cloth, a basket or a paper bag, and a sharp knife. But don't let your rapture at discovering a fine clump of gilled fungi, or puffballs, or shaggymanes, allow you to pull them up carelessly and throw them helter-skelter into the basket or paper bag. You need to be sure not only of the *kinds* you pick but of their *age* and *condition*. Avoid those that are old, limp, and flabby, for in all probability they have already been partly decomposed by bacteria, and some of these bacteria or their decomposition products may be harmful. When you have selected a ripe, plump specimen, cut off the stem neatly just above the ground. Then wipe the cap with your cloth and remove from the under surface any debris that may be present. Ordinarily the gills are clean, but small beetles or an occasional slug may have got in among them. These interlopers should be removed on the spot, even though you are intending to make a spore print when you get home.

Now that you are certain that the outside of the mushroom is clean, break open the cap, split the stem lengthwise, and examine each one for the presence of fly or beetle larvae. If only the stem is infested, it can be broken off and discarded, but if you find maggots in the cap by all means throw it away. When the mushroom has thus passed inspection, put it in your bag or basket. It is well to segregate the tender and tough kinds, perhaps by making a paper partition in your basket or by taking along an extra paper bag, for you have to sort them anyway before cooking them.

After you have brought the mushrooms home, remember that many of those with gills can be safely identified only by making a spore print of *each individual*. Young specimens of Agaricus, Amanita, and Lepiota, for example, are difficult to recognize until the caps have expanded sufficiently to allow the gills to release the spores. But fungi that can be unmistakably identified by shape, color, or similar obvious characters can be cooked immediately. In fact, shaggymanes and inky caps cannot be kept, even in a refrigerator, because of their peculiar liquefying habit. Others, after being properly identified, can be kept in a cold, dry place until you are ready to use them.

You may feel at this point, after so many warnings and cautions, that hunting wild mushrooms to eat is a grim and dangerous business. But the author guarantees — as can the thousands of amateur mycologists and mushroom epicures all over this country — that one excursion into the woods and fields, one dish of these most delicious and succulent of all foods (simply and quickly prepared according to any of the recipes in the last section of this book) will transform whatever fears you may have had into a lasting enthusiasm!

When you have reached this stage you may want to keep a notebook in which you can record the kind and quantity of the different mushrooms you have found, the dates on which you found them, their locations, and on what kinds of soil, what trees or stumps, they were growing. The experience you acquire in this way will be worth any amount of book learning, and if you keep the records accurately over a period of years they may be of real scientific value. Since the mycelium from which the mushrooms arise is relatively permanent, once you have learned where certain kinds abound you will probably have assured yourself of a supply for many years to come.

Sample Data Sheet

DATE: 9/24/42

LOCALITY: Hamline Ave. and County Road F. In oak woods 200 yards in from the northeast corner of the intersection.

MUSHROOMS FOUND: *Puffballs:* abundant on logs, but too old to be edible; should look a few weeks earlier next year.

Sulphur shelf fungus: several specimens on oak trees, some young and fresh enough to eat.

Honey fungus: numerous fresh young clumps around old stumps.

Several others, not identified.

The Foolproof Four

From the more than fifty common edible mushrooms described in this book, we have selected four kinds as being the most easily and surely recognized, most abundant and widespread, and most desirable in flavor and texture. All four have definite characteristics that positively distinguish them from doubtful, inedible, or poisonous kinds, and even from other edible kinds. Once he learns their few distinguishing marks the beginner can gather and eat these mushrooms without fear or hesitation and with the assurance that wherever he may be he is enjoying the best that mushrooms have to offer. All are common throughout much of the United States and Canada; all rank high in edibility and lend themselves to varied ways of preparation. They are among the elite of the mushroom world.

All four of these mushrooms are also described and illustrated in the following section, but a brief, concise synopsis of each should be especially valuable to the beginner who wishes to be sure of a few kinds before he has gained the experience and confidence that will enable him to know the others equally well. The experienced mycologist, too, can use this section to initiate his friends into a fascinating pursuit.

Morels, or Sponge Mushrooms

The illustrations (Figure 1 and Plate 4F) show the general shape of morels far better than words can describe it, and although the several different kinds of morels differ somewhat in shape and size, nobody who has seen even a picture of one can confuse morels with any other plant. The irregular pits and ridges of the cap are the distinguishing feature. The plant stands from 2 to 6 inches high, the cap forming the upper half or two thirds and the stem the remainder. The cap is tan to brown, the stem somewhat paler, and

Figure 1. A group of morels growing in leaf mold behind a garage at Sacaton, Arizona. Photo by John T. Presley.

both stem and cap are hollow and brittle in texture. Look for morels in the woods every spring, from February in the southern United States to late May in the North, the time of appearance varying, of course, with the weather. Morels are unexcelled when cooked, and they can also be dried easily and saved for future use.

Puffballs

Although the most important species of puffballs are discussed in greater detail in the next section, for our purpose here puffballs may be best described as follows: They grow on the ground or on rotten wood and logs; they are white in color, roughly spherical in shape or with a round head that tapers down to a narrower base. (See Figures 2 and 3 and Plate 1D). In size they vary from those smaller than a golf ball to those a foot or more in diameter. When the ball is split from top to bottom the interior is uniformly firm and white. In such a section there may be a basal portion that differs slightly in texture from the head proper, although this rudimentary

Figure 2. Pear-shaped puffballs common on decaying wood. As the spines mature, they fall off.

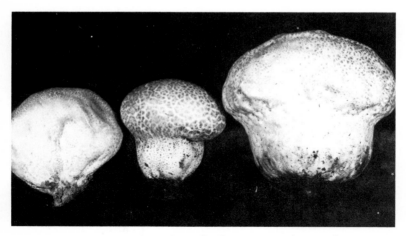

Figure 3. Vase-shaped puffballs common in meadows.

stem is not found in all puffballs. If a *definite and distinct stem* runs through such a section from bottom to top, the plant is *not* a puffball!

Puffballs can be found in open, grassy meadows and parks and among hardwood trees and brush. They occur all through the growing season but are likely to be far more abundant in the fall. Like many other kinds of mushrooms they come up in the same place year after year, and when sliced and fried in butter they have few rivals. The only simple precautions to be observed are, first, to examine the interior closely for evidence of tiny worms, which may infest the base and work up through the body of the puffball, rendering it unfit for food; and, second, to eat only those that are firm and white inside. Once the interior begins to turn yellow the puffball is not desirable for food, although by no means poisonous.

Sulphur Shelf Mushrooms, or Sulphur Polypores

These mushrooms (Figure 4) belong to the general group of wood-inhabiting shelf fungi. They grow on old rotten logs and on standing trees, both living and dead. Oaks are their favorite host, but they are found on a large variety of other trees as well and are common throughout the country.

On fallen logs the sulphur polypore forms colorful orange and yellow rosettes of many overlapping, fan-shaped shelves. On standing trees the shelves appear one above the other, often for a distance of several feet up and down the trunk. Clumps weighing several pounds are not uncommon. The shelves extend from 4 to 10 inches outward from the point where the base is attached to the wood. In fresh specimens the upper surface is zoned with yellow and bright golden orange and the lower surface is bright yellow, but upon exposure to weather the upper surface gradually fades to a more or less uniform pale yellow. The lower surface is composed of a layer of fine pores, whence the name polypore.

The sulphur polypore is to be sought in the fall wherever old decaying trees abound. The shape and color make it impossible to confuse this species with any other mushroom, and when properly cooked it will provide a delicious meal. Incidentally, it decays the interior of the trees it inhabits, reducing the heartwood to a brown charcoal-like mass. Once clumps of it have been located one can confidently expect it to fruit again in the same place year after year — a point worth remembering.

Figure 4. Sulphur shelf on a rotten log.

Shaggymanes

These luscious mushrooms (Figure 5 and Plate 1B) are the best of the eminently edible inky-cap group, whose distinguishing mark is the dissolution of the ripening cap into a black liquid, as illustrated in Figure 52. The shaggymane is usually from 4 to 6 inches high, although we have found giant ones more than 20 inches tall and weighing easily half a pound. The cap is nearly cylindrical, white and shaggy, with large brownish pointed tufts. In young specimens there is a narrow, loose ring around the stem just at the lower edge of the cap, but this soon withers and disappears.

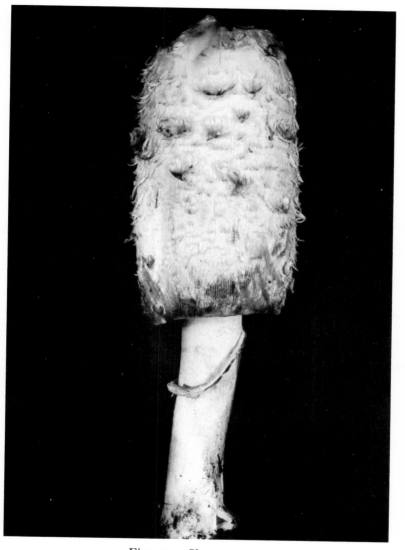

Figure 5. Shaggymane.

23

As with morels, the general shape of the shaggymane is so characteristic (see Plate 1B) that if you have seen a good illustration of it you cannot fail to recognize it on sight. Normally shaggymanes grow in groups of a few to several dozen on lawns, along boulevards, in grassy parks and fields in town and country from spring until fall, and they often come up in the same place year after year. If the lower edge of the cap has begun to turn black it should be cut away before cooking. Shaggymanes cannot be kept for more than a few hours, unfortunately, even in a refrigerator, because they continue to ripen and are transformed rather rapidly into a black liquid.

Mushrooms with Gills

White Spore Print

Those who eat mushrooms are again warned that to learn the common poisonous species and avoid them and to eat all others is risking serious illness or death! The edibility of all species is not known. The only safe procedure is to learn *thoroughly* a few of the common edible ones and to avoid all others. The purpose of including some of the more common poisonous kinds in this book is to show how these resemble, and how they can be distinguished from, the common edible kinds.

The genus Amanita, named for Amanos, a mountain in Asia Minor, contains the more common deadly species of mushrooms. These may be identified by the following characteristics. Learn them well!

1. White spores.

2. Gills that are free from the stem; that is, they extend almost to the stem but do not touch it.

3. A ring around the upper part of the stem. In newly expanded specimens this is always visible and usually prominent, but it often collapses, withers, and disappears in older specimens. The stem should be examined very closely for evidence of it.

4. A cup, or volva, surrounding the base of the stem. In some species this is beneath the surface of the ground or buried in leaf litter or grass and thus will be missed unless one carefully digs up the entire stem. Moreover, this cup also withers and almost disappears with age.

To make identification even more difficult, the volva, instead of being always a definite cup-like structure enclosing the base of the stem, is sometimes merely a series of partial and inconspicuous rings on the swollen base of the stem, permitting confusion with the genus Lepiota and even with young specimens of Agaricus. The prominent and movable ring on the stem of *Lepiota procera* and its scaly cap enable one to distinguish it readily from any Amanitas, and the pink gills of young specimens of Agaricus and the purple spores and gills of mature specimens permit positive identification, but species about which one is in doubt *should not be eaten!*

Fortunately, few species of Amanita are very common outside the forested areas, but even the most deadly ones are found now and again almost wherever wild mushrooms grow.*

Poisonous: AMANITA PHALLOIDES (Death Cap)

This deadly species (Figure 6) has been blamed for a large proportion of the cases of fatal mushroom poisoning, since it is fairly common throughout the North Temperate Zone in America and Europe. Even a small piece is sufficient to cause serious illness or death. A clinical account of the death of four persons from amanitine poisoning is quoted in *Mushrooms and Toadstools* by Güssow and Odell, one of the references cited on page 119. A careful reading of the progress of the poisoning, through all stages from cramping pains and delirium to painful death, should serve as sufficient warning to hasty or careless mushroom hunters. It is easy enough to learn and to bear in mind the unmistakable Amanita characteristics — so easy that to ignore them is unforgivable.

Several varieties of *A. phalloides* occur, differing chiefly in color, size, and some microscopic characters. The cap is from 2 to 6 inches wide, a pale grayish brown near the center but nearly white toward the margin, convex when young and later sloping downward from the center like an inverted saucer; in old specimens the margin is raised up slightly above the rest of the cap. The surface is sticky when moist, but in dry weather it must be dampened to reveal this quality. Often on newly expanded caps, soft, white, warty patches of mycelium are scattered over the surface, but these soon disappear. The gills are white and do not touch the stem, being free as in Lepiota and Agaricus. The

* The first-aid procedure for any poison taken by mouth is to have the stomach pumped or to induce vomiting as soon as possible. Call your doctor!

flesh is about 1/4 inch thick near the stem, white, firm, and brittle in fresh specimens but rather soft and limp in old ones. At the top the stem is 1/4 inch or more in thickness, increasing in diameter toward the base, and is white and brittle. The spherical base is buried beneath the surface of the ground; therefore the soft white volva surrounding it is usually visible only if one digs up the whole plant. The veil that connects the edge of the young, unexpanded cap with the stem breaks as the cap expands and forms a ring on the stem. This ring is at first fairly prominent and has narrow, parallel, radial furrows on the upper side, but it soon withers and eventually may disappear completely.

In other words, of the two characteristics usually cited as typical of the genus Amanita the *volva* of this species is concealed beneath the surface of the ground and can easily be missed, and the *ring* is evanescent, being visible as a definite ring only in comparatively fresh young specimens.

Figure 6. *Amanita phalloides* (Death Cap). Poisonous. Figure 7. *A. verna.* Poisonous. The ring has already disappeared from the one on the left.

Figure 8. *Amanita verna*. Poisonous.

In books one sees only perfect and so-called typical specimens; in nature, however, one finds them growing under widely varying circumstances, and therefore when they have become partially crushed beneath logs, stones, or other debris or when part of the cap has been torn away in emerging from the soil or when they have passed maturity, it is not always possible to identify them with certainty.

Poisonous: AMANITA VERNA

Amanita verna (Figures 7 and 8) is considered by some to be not a separate species but a variety of *A. phalloides,* the chief difference being that its cap is pure white. In the northern Lake States *A. verna* is very abundant almost every fall, and on a morning's walk one can see literally thousands of beautiful and stately white specimens, growing singly and in groups of three or four, especially in aspen woods and hazel brush. It is a beautiful plant, but deadly. Although both species are more common in forested regions, they are by no means restricted to these areas.

Poisonous: AMANITA MUSCARIA (Fly Agaric)

The species name is taken from the name of the common housefly, *Musca domestica,* because the fungus has a peculiar and fatal attraction for these busy and annoying pests. If pieces of *A. muscaria* (Figures 9 and 10) are broken up and placed in a shal-

Figure 9. *Amanita muscaria* (Fly Agaric). Poisonous.
Photo by Frank H. Kaufert.

31

Figure 10. A close-up view of *Amanita muscaria*. Poisonous.
Photo by Frank H. Kaufert.

low saucer of water, houseflies soon begin to cluster around, eager for a tipple. It is their last. In a few moments, seemingly stimulated by this too potent elixir, they take off and buzz about in frenzied loops and circles until sudden death overtakes them, often in full flight, and they tumble quite lifeless to the floor. But flies are not the only creatures susceptible to the peculiar attractions of this fungus, for in some regions of Siberia it was once, and probably still is, commonly used as an intoxicant by man, nonlethal doses of it producing a temporarily glorious binge. The after-effects are less joyous, involving rather severe aches and pains, but these do not seem to have deterred its use. *Eaten in quantity, of course, it is fatal.*

This is one of the largest, most colorful, and most imposing of gill fungi. Specimens more than a foot high with caps 10 inches wide have been found several times by the author and doubtless by many others. In dense forests of mixed hardwoods we have come upon large fairy rings made up of perfect specimens approaching this size, and with their brightly colored caps they made an impressive sight.

The average cap is from 6 to 8 inches wide, and the *color varies from straw-yellow to reddish orange,* the reddish shades being more typical. The surface is spotted with *large white or pale yellow warts* that are likely to be distributed in circles, but these warts may be shed from old specimens. The gills are white or very pale yellow and scarcely touch the stem. The flesh is white, spongy, and brittle. The stem is from 1/4 to 1/2 inch wide at the top, gradually increasing in diameter toward the bulbous base. The soft, white ring is at first very conspicuous but soon dries and disappears. The volva typically shows up only as a *series of partial ridges on the bulbous base of the stem;* that is, there is no true volva but only a hint or suggestion of one. This species has more than once been mistaken for *Amanita caesaria,* one of the few edible species of Amanita, which is fortunately more common in Southern Europe than here.

Poisonous: AMANITA RUSSULOIDES

Though not so common as the two preceding species, this one is found in large numbers during the late spring and summer of certain years. It is supposedly, but not certainly, poisonous and *should by all means be avoided.* We have found it in scattered colonies in deciduous forests, but it is not likely to appear in the same place every year.

The plants are sturdy and attractive, as the illustrations indicate (see Figure 11 and Plate 3B), with caps from about 4 to 6 inches wide, straw-yellow or nearly white, very sticky when fresh and moist, and bearing *thick, soft, white warts* that look almost artificial. As the plants age, the caps become quite flat, the specimen pictured being still in the prime of life. The *edge of the cap is marked with prominent radial ridges.* In large specimens the stem

Figure 11. *Amanita russuloides*. Poisonous.

34

may be 8 inches long and 1/2 inch thick and typically is tapered slightly or not at all. It bears a ring that is at first definite and distinct but soon withers, and its enlarged base tapers to a blunt point in the ground. Sometimes the margin of the cup is clear cut, but more often it forms only broken rings on the stem.

GENUS Amanitopsis

Edible but not recommended: AMANITOPSIS VAGINATA

The fact that the generic name means resembling Amanita is a warning to all amateur mushroom enthusiasts. This genus differs from Amanita chiefly in not having a ring on the stem, but since this ring may disappear from the stem of overmature specimens of Amanita, the two may be confused by beginners. Therefore Amanitopsis, although edible, is not recommended for eating.

There are several species, of which *A. vaginata* (Figure 12) is the most common, a plant of delicately graceful beauty, growing almost throughout the country in wooded places during summer and fall. Several varieties are known, differing in the color of the cap, the more common one being white, another mouse-gray, another orange. All have free gills and white gills and spores.

The cap is flat and from 2 to 4 inches wide, with prominent ridges at the margin. The stem is from 4 to 8 inches long, white and brittle. The base of the stem, with the surrounding sheath that suggests the species name, is buried an inch or two in the soil, and unless one suspects the presence of a volva and carefully digs it up with a knife or trowel, it is likely to be missed.

GENUS Armillaria

Eminently edible: ARMILLARIA MELLEA (Honey, or Shoestring, Fungus)

Armillaria is derived from a Latin word meaning a ring and refers to the ring on the stem of mushrooms in this genus, but the

Figure 12. *Amanitopsis vaginata*. Edible but not recommended.

name is not altogether fitting because the ring is often inconspicuous or even absent in all but very young specimens. *Mellea,* meaning honey-like, is descriptive of the color of the fungus, not the
taste. The species is characterized by (1) white spores, (2) gills
that taper downward on the stem, and (3) a delicate, cottony ring
connecting the cap and stem of young plants.

Like other organisms that grow under many different conditions it varies a great deal, and even after one has known and
gathered it for years he continually meets forms that differ just a
little from the type (Figure 13 and Plate 2D).

A. mellea is interesting not only because of its variability but
because it has frequently been suspected of being a menace to
orchard, forest, and shade trees, rotting the roots and thus killing
the trees. Normally it lives on dead roots and other woody debris
and spreads by means of black, string-like aggregations of mycelium (whence the name *shoestring*) that grow through the soil
from one root to another. One of these strings may invade the root
of a living tree by growing directly through the bark, and once
inside it spreads out in the soft wood underneath, killing the tissues
as it advances. At the same time it grows into and rots the wood
of the root, reducing it to a white, stringy or spongy pulp. It also
advances up into the trunk of the tree, causing a fairly common
heart rot in both shade and forest trees. The decayed wood is
usually luminescent, glowing in the dark with a pale yellow light —
an eerie enough sight to come upon of a rainy night!

The fruit bodies almost always come up in clumps, often in such
numbers and so close together as literally to cover the earth. In
a recently cutover woodland in central Minnesota the author
counted five hundred fruit bodies in an area twelve feet square,
amounting to at least a bushel in volume, and they were only
slightly less numerous in other patches scattered over several acres.
On our lawn in St. Paul hundreds of them have formed an almost
solid carpet about three feet wide and thirty feet long, apparently
nourished by the decayed root of an oak cut down many years ago.

The most common variety is rather squat, with a pale brown

Figure 13. *Armillaria mellea* (Honey, or Shoestring, Fungus).
Eminently edible.

or honey-colored cap from 2 to 4 inches wide, convex and bearing many small, pointed brown scales or tufts that are very numerous near the center and thus make it seem darker. When fresh and young, the cap is slimy or sticky, and if old, dry caps are soaked in water for a few minutes this sliminess reappears. The margin of young specimens is curved inward toward the stem and connected to it by a delicate, cottony veil in which each strand of mycelium is visible. This delicate veil remains for a short time as a ring near the top of the stem, but it soon withers and disappears. The gills are white, sometimes with a faint tinge of tan, and extend from 1/8 to 1/4 inch down the stem. The flesh of the cap is firm and white. The stem is from 2 to 6 inches long and 1/2 inch thick, colored like the cap, twisted and fibrous; it splits lengthwise very readily.

The color of the cap in other varieties ranges from yellow to dark brown. Some giant specimens were found in 1938 near Lake

38

Vadnais, on the outskirts of St. Paul, with caps more than 8 inches wide and with stems 1 inch thick and more than 12 inches long. Those found in grassy places around old oak stumps are likely to be rather squat, with stems from 2 to 4 inches long, and these usually grow so close together that many of the caps are distorted. Because large quantities of this mushroom appear in the fall, it is a favorite for canning. A winter's supply often springs up around an old stump or above dead roots in the yard or garden. It often appears after rather severe frosts, being one of the last to be found abundantly in the fall.

GENUS Cantharellus

This generic name, taken from a Greek word meaning vase, is an apt one because of the narrow, flaring shape of the common species. All species of Cantharellus are edible; in Europe some are collected in quantity and sold in the public markets.

The gills run a good way down the stem, are prominently and irregularly forked, and in several species are so thick that they are little more than ridges. Only the two species common enough and large enough to be of importance from a standpoint of edibility will be described.

Edible: CANTHARELLUS AURANTIACUS

The caps and gills are *orange-yellow or golden yellow*, the cap being from 2 to 4 inches wide and *shaped like an irregular, shallow funnel* (Figure 14). The *gills are forked* even more than appears in the picture. The stem is reddish brown, short, and rather thick. It is fairly common in the fall, arising singly and in groups of two or three from the ground or from very rotten wood.

Eminently edible: CANTHARELLUS CIBARIUS

The *funnel-shaped cap*, with the margin curved down, the *thick, much forked gills*, the *short, tapering stem*, and the *bright chrome-*

39

Figure 14. *Cantharellus aurantiacus*. Edible.

Figure 15. *Cantharellus cibarius*. Eminently edible.

yellow color make this plant almost impossible to confuse with any other (Figure 15 and Plate 4D). It is found over a wide range in both coniferous and hardwood forests, and in texture and flavor it can be rated well above the average edible mushroom. It is a prime favorite in both Europe and America.

GENUS Clitocybe

The genus name, meaning sloping head, describes the funnel-shaped cap of some species. It is distinguished by (1) white spores, (2) unforked gills that run down the stem a short distance, and (3) a somewhat tough or fibrous stem. No ring or cup is present. There are many species, some of them abundant but of unknown edibility, others known to be edible, and at least one known fairly certainly to be poisonous.

Unwholesome or poisonous: CLITOCYBE ILLUDENS
(Jack-o'-Lantern)

Because of its luminescent glow at night this mushroom has been given its common name. The plants are striking in appearance (Figure 16 and Plate 3A), the cap, gills, and stem being a *bright orange-yellow*, later fading to yellow. *Numerous tall fruit bodies arise in a clump*, the stems curving gracefully upward and outward from a common point of origin on a stump or log, the whole making a gay splash of color against the gray wood. As stated above, *the fruit bodies are luminescent*, and on rainy nights clumps of them at the bases of stumps can be seen for some distance, a sight not likely to instill confidence into the hearts of those to whom the woods after dark are strange and fearsome!

The caps are from 3 to 4 inches in diameter, slightly convex, curving downward from the center toward the margin, often with a little rounded or pointed bump in the center. The bright yellow gills taper downward on the stem for 1/4 inch or more. The stem is from 1/3 to 1/2 inch in diameter, 5 to 8 inches long, yellow or orange, curved, and tapering to a point at the base, where the numerous stems of a clump come together.

These mushrooms are probably not deadly poisonous, but they will cause violent illness. Some years ago in the fall several of them were brought in to the University of Minnesota by a man who said he had collected a bushel and wanted to know if they were

Figure 16. *Clitocybe illudens* (Jack-o'-Lantern).
Unwholesome or poisonous.

edible. When told they were likely to be poisonous he said he had eaten some a day or two before, with no ill effects, and intended to can the rest for winter use. One can only recommend so enthusiastic a mushroom eater to the protection of a kind providence. Because the specimens were rather tough he had boiled them for about an hour in water and had then discarded the water. The poison is apparently soluble in water and can be removed in this way — for which he should be thankful!

Edible: CLITOCYBE LACCATA

This common species (Figure 17 and Plate 4C) is found almost everywhere in wooded areas from early spring until late fall. Though it usually comes up in clusters, it may occur singly also. The cap of young specimens is convex, later becoming flat, and about 1 to 1 1/2 inches across. The colors of both cap and gills are exceedingly variable, the most common being a light salmon, but

Figure 17. *Clitocybe laccata.* Edible.

those with a watery red cap and lilac or even purple gills are by no means rare. The color of the cap fades rapidly as it dries.

The peculiar *mealy texture of its surface* and the characteristic *waxy appearance of the gills* serve more than color to identify the species. The gills are thick and rather far apart and, where they are attached to the cap, are connected by a network of ridges that can easily be seen by looking at a specimen from the under side. Only by making a spore print could one unfamiliar with them learn the spore color of this species.

43

GENUS Collybia

The name Collybia, derived from a Greek word meaning a small coin, probably refers to the regular, disc-shaped cap of some of the species. The genus may be distinguished by (1) white spores, (2) gills that vary from being almost free to being attached to the stem but do not descend the stem at all, (3) the rather tough stem, and (4) the inrolled margin of the cap of young specimens. Of the comparatively large number of species only four will be described. Many of the species are difficult to identify, and few are especially good to eat.

Edible: COLLYBIA CONFLUENS

The species name means growing together and is descriptive of the habits of the plant (Figure 18). A regular inhabitant of the northern forests, this species has usurped the so-called reviving habit of the genus Marasmius; that is, in dry weather the fruit bodies wilt and shrivel but do not collapse, and with the advent of rain they again expand, as is shown in the before-and-after study on the following page.

The whole plant is pale brown when moist and light tan when dry, the gills being almost the same color as the cap. The stems, *covered with a frosty bloom of hair,* are very *tough and fibrous and in older specimens are hollow.* Unfortunately the flesh tends to retain this toughness when cooked. The caps average only about 1 inch in diameter, although many are smaller, and the stems are 3 or 4 inches long. However, this diminutive mushroom can be collected in quantities since it grows in clumps that are often scattered rather thickly over the forest floor.

Edible: COLLYBIA PLATYPHYLLA (Broad-gilled Collybia)

The *unusually wide gills* of this fungus, the *thick, tough, twisted white stem,* combined with its *habit of growing on wood,* set it apart from most other species (Figure 20 and Plate 2C). It is a

44

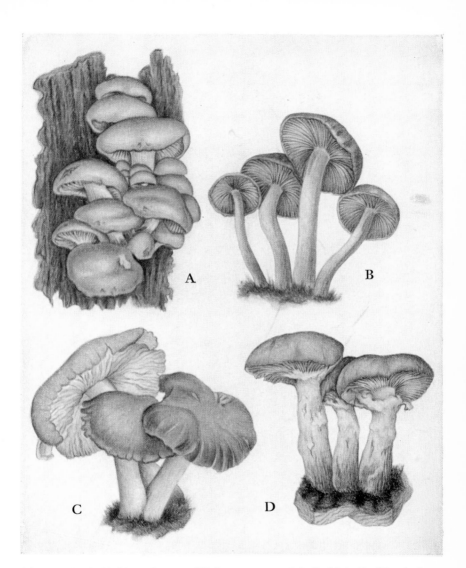

Plate 2. A. *Collybia velutipes* (Velvet-stemmed Collybia). B. *Hypholoma sublateritium* (Brick-red Hypholoma). C. *Collybia platyphylla* (Broad-gilled Collybia). D. *Armillaria mellea* (Honey Fungus). All edible.

Figure 18. *Collybia confluens*. Edible. The clump on the left is dry and shriveled. Those on the right were the same size as those on the left, but they revived when moistened. Figure 19. C. *radicata* (Rooted Collybia). Edible.

Figure 20. *Collybia platyphylla* (Broad-gilled Collybia). Edible.

45

large plant, with caps from 3 to 6 inches wide and stems from 1/2 to 1 inch in diameter and from 4 to 6 inches long. The upper surface of the cap is grayish brown in the center, paler toward the margin, and delicately streaked with dark radial fibers. The gills are quite white, rather far apart, and from 3/4 to 1 inch wide; in young specimens they are attached to the stem but may break away from it as the cap expands. It grows on rotten wood, the interior of old hollow stumps being a favorite habitat, and comes up singly or in groups of two or three.

Edible: COLLYBIA RADICATA (Rooted Collybia)

This rooting Collybia (Figure 19), though never present in large numbers, can almost always be found in wooded areas from spring until fall. The cap is from 2 to 4 inches wide, dark tan all over or dark in the center and paler toward the margin, with dark radial fibers running out from the center to the margin, as in the preceding species. In moist weather the tops of fresh specimens are covered with a thick layer of an almost mucilaginous substance, but this dries up when the humidity is low. The gills are white, somewhat farther apart than they are in most gilled fungi, and attached to the stem.

The slender stem may be only 1/3 inch in diameter and 6 inches or more in length. Surprisingly enough the stem does not end at or just beneath the surface of the ground, as in most other mushrooms, but continues as a tapering black root for 6 or 8 inches, straight down. This root is *the most reliable character by which the species can be recognized*, but care must be used to avoid breaking the stem at the ground level, thus missing the subterranean part.

Eminently edible: COLLYBIA VELUTIPES (Velvet-stemmed Collybia)

The accuracy of the species name, *velutipes*, meaning velvet stem, proves that scientists are not always occupied with making

Figure 21. *Collybia velutipes* (Velvet-stemmed Collybia).
Eminently edible.

nature incomprehensible! This is a mushroom all should know (Figure 21 and Plate 2A), since it is very common, growing in bright reddish brown clumps out of old branch stubs and wounds on shade and forest trees. It is one of the first to appear in the spring and one of the last to disappear in the fall. In fact, it is so tenacious of life that individuals emerging in late autumn may endure through the winter, even in severe climates, and on warm January days they will pop up in all their colorful freshness, leading those who do not know the habits of the species to believe that the fruit body has developed in the dead of winter.

The caps are at first reddish brown, later tan, and in moist weather they will shine with a light reflected from their sticky, gelatinous surface. Fully expanded caps vary from 1 1/2 to 3 inches in diameter. The gills are white, narrow, and close together.

The stems are from 1/4 to 1/2 inch in diameter and 2 to 5 inches long, several or many arising from the same spot and curving outward and upward. When young they are somewhat paler than the caps and tinged with yellow, but as they age they become covered toward the base *with a dense, velvety pile of reddish brown hairs.*

The edibility of this plant is excellent — which may in part condone the damage it does by rotting the interior of our trees. Basswood is a favorite host, but it is found on other hardwoods also.

GENUS Lactarius

This genus is normally one of the most easily recognized, for the name, meaning milky, is descriptive of the white or colored juice that exudes from the flesh of the cap or gills when they are broken. In dry weather this telltale juice may be scanty or even wanting altogether in some species, but if so-called mushroom weather prevails, one need only bend back the cap enough to break the edges of a few gills in order to see the bead-like drops of juice ooze out. Subjected to such a test, a mushroom that *exudes droplets of a white or colored liquid* is invariably Lactarius, although, as stated above, a Lactarius does not always provide this evidence of its identity.

The flesh of the cap is unusually brittle, never tough or stringy. There are many species; almost all are fairly large and share a common shape — squat, with a shallow, funnel-like cap and a thick, short stem. Their colors may run through the hues of the rainbow, and they vary in edibility from choice to undesirable. A few rare species are even suspected of being poisonous. Many have a sharp and bitter taste when fresh, but Güssow and Odell report that several species previously considered poisonous because of this taste are edible and delicious, since the objectionable flavor disappears when the mushrooms are cooked.

Edible: LACTARIUS CILICIOIDES

This species (Figure 22) illustrates the typical Lactarius shape. It is from 4 to 6 inches wide, about the same in height; the upper surface is white, or alternately banded in tan and white, and sticky; the inrolled margin or the entire surface is *covered with densely matted hairs.*

The juice is rather scanty, white but turning pale yellow almost as soon as it is exposed to the air (this is especially noticeable where gills and flesh join) and in a few minutes becoming white again. It is fairly common, especially in coniferous woods, in late summer and fall, individual specimens being scattered through the forest.

Eminently edible: LACTARIUS DELICIOSUS

This species (Figure 23) has the shape and size more or less characteristic of the genus, being about 4 to 5 inches both in width and in height. In color it is fairly amazing; the upper surface is pale orange, fading to tan with age, and is often zoned with broad concentric bands of pale orange and tan. The gills are reddish orange, becoming green with age or when bruised, and the yellow or orange juice is produced copiously, droplets of it standing out in sharp contrast to the greenish gills of old specimens. The short, thick stem is colored like the cap and becomes green where one

49

Figure 22. *Lactarius cilicioides*. Edible.

Figure 23. *Lactarius deliciosus*. Eminently edible.

touches it. In spite of its rather disconcerting array of colors the fungus is, as its name implies, delicious. It is a fall plant and can be found scattered on the ground in forests, sometimes in considerable numbers.

Figure 24. *Lactarius subdulcis*. Edible.

Edible: LACTARIUS SUBDULCIS

This is one of the smaller species of the genus (Figure 24 and Plate 4B), but it amply makes up in numbers for its lack of size. The fruit body is a uniform reddish brown, the caps being from 1 to 2 inches wide and the stems from 2 to 2 1/2 inches long and somewhat slender, at least for a Lactarius. The top of the cap is flat or nearly so, with a small rounded bump just above the stem, and the surface has a slightly mealy appearance.

The juice is white and often rather scanty, but it can usually be seen when the cap is bent back far enough to split the edges of the gills. The species is common in fields and woods from spring until fall, almost invariably appearing in groups of a dozen or more. Patches containing a hundred are not uncommon.

GENUS Hypomyces

Edible but not recommended: HYPOMYCES LACTI-FLUORUM

Figure 25. *Hypomyces lacti-fluorum.* Edible but not recommended.

This species is so distinctive (see Figure 25) that once recognized it can scarcely be mistaken for any other. When it first pushes up through the leaf mold *the entire fruit body is bright orange* and remains so until it begins to decay, when the color deepens to *orange-red or dark red.*

The caps are from 3 to 6 inches wide, and in general shaped like *shallow funnels with their edges curved down,* but they often are twisted into curious and tortured variations of this form. The thick cap tapers to a thick stem, which may be as much as 4 or 5 inches long but is often so short as scarcely to be a stem at all. *No gills are present,* their place being taken by thick ridges. The entire cap and stem are *covered with tiny pimples,* each with a *pinpoint of red* in the center. When the cap is broken open the orange color is seen to be confined to a thin outer layer, the interior being white and firm.

This monstrosity, for so it is, is the result of a combination of two different fungi. The main body of the plant, represented by the white interior, is composed of the tissue of a true gilled mushroom. The outer, brightly colored layer is a parasitic fungus closely related to some common molds, and the whole represents a good example of one fungus causing a disease on another. The small pimples on the surface are the protruding snouts of innumerable fruit bodies of the parasite; through these snouts the spores of the parasite are discharged with some force. So numerous are they that if a specimen is left covered on a piece of paper over night the discharged spores will form a powdery white deposit easily 1/10 inch deep.

The parasitized gill fungus is said to be *Lactarius piperatus*, a perfectly edible mushroom. The parasite itself is also edible. However, since the author has seen these parasitized plants sometimes growing near *Russula delica*, it seems likely that the parasite may attack more than one species of gilled fungus. If this is true, one cannot be certain of the identity of the mushroom after recognizing the parasite, and therefore the species could scarcely be recommended as good eating. It is listed as edible in various texts, and it has been generally eaten throughout the northern part of this country, where it grows. But those the author has eaten were not of particularly good flavor, nor was the night one of sweet and dreamless sleep!

GENUS Lentinus

Edible: LENTINUS LEPIDEUS

The generic name means tough, and tough these fungi are. The only common species, *L. lepideus* (meaning scaly) is a cosmopolitan plant that thrives wherever coniferous timber is found (Figure 26). It grows on, and decays, the wood of pine, spruce, larch, and other conifers, and seems to prefer railroad ties, bridge timbers, and so on, although it is by no means uncommon in the woods on old logs and stumps.

The cap is from 3 to 5 inches wide, white with coarse, flat brown scales distributed roughly

Figure 26. *Lentinus lepideus.* Edible.

in concentric circles, and it varies in shape from uniformly convex to convex with a depression in the center. The flesh is tough and white. The wide, white gills run a short way down the stem and have prominently saw-toothed edges. There is a faint ring just below the gills, but this soon disappears and one must find fresh young specimens to see it at all plainly. The stem is either smooth or scaly, from 1/4 to 3/4 inch wide and from 2 to 6 inches long. When fresh the plant has a faint but characteristic *odor suggesting licorice*, and this odor, combined with the *saw-toothed gill edges, the tough texture, and growth on wood*, makes identification relatively certain. It endures for weeks and because of its firmness can be grated to flavor gravies and other foods.

GENUS Lenzites

Edible but tough: LENZITES BETULINA

The genus, named after Lenz, a German botanist, is characterized by (1) the stemless cap, (2) the exceedingly tough, leathery

Figure 27. *Lenzites betulina.* Edible but tough.

texture, (3) the gills, which are just as tough as the cap and often interbranched to form pores, and (4) its growth on wood.

This particular species (Figure 27) is exceedingly common on old birch and aspen logs, growing in rather large clusters, as the illustration indicates. The caps are 1 or 2 inches wide and from 1/4 to 1/2 inch thick where they are attached to the wood on which they grow. The upper side in fresh specimens is woolly and beautifully zoned in orange, gray, and tan. Though edible, this species is far too tough and leathery to be relished.

GENUS Lepiota

The genus name, meaning scaly, is descriptive of the surface of the caps in many species. The genus is characterized by (1) white spores, (2) free gills, (3) a definite ring around the stem, and (4) the fact that the stem separates readily from the cap — such definite characteristics that it is ordinarily one of the easiest genera for a beginner to recognize. In shape and size as well as in other features these mushrooms resemble the deadly genus Amanita, but they differ in that the stem parts from the cap easily and cleanly when worked this way and that.

Two of the three species here described, *Lepiota procera* and *Lepiota rachodes*, are edible, but *L. rachodes* resembles *Lepiota morgani* so closely that any beginner should avoid it. *L. morgani* is poisonous, and mushroom hunters with years of experience have often mistaken it for *Lepiota rachodes*, eaten it, and become dangerously ill. This is another example of the need for extreme caution in eating mushrooms about whose identity there is the slightest doubt and of the danger run by people who do not distinguish between what they *believe* they know and what they *know* they know.

Young plants of *Lepiota morgani* might also be confused with Agaricus, especially if the two come up near one another, as they sometimes do. For this reason, if you pick young mushrooms having (1) a definite veil or ring, (2) free gills, and (3) white gills, do not eat them until you have made a spore print of each.

Edible: LEPIOTA PROCERA (Parasol Mushroom)

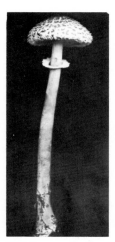

Figure 28. *Lepiota procera.* (Parasol Mushroom). Edible.

The specific name means tall, but to do the plant justice the word stately really should be added to its description (Figure 28). It comes up in the fall in pastures and open hardwood forests, and a troop of these tall, graceful white plants is a sight one need not be a naturalist to enjoy. They often stand a foot high, each tapering stem supporting a cap 4 to 6 inches or more in width. The cap is at first rounded, with the margin attached to the stem, but later it becomes almost flat, with a round hump in the center. The surface is white, marked with gradually diminishing circles of prominent brown scales. A thick ring surrounds the upper part of the stem; this ring can be moved up and down and often falls by its own weight to the base. The white gills do not touch the stem at all. The flesh is also white. The *movable ring* on the stem, the *length of the stem* in relation to the width of the cap, and the *stately proportions of the entire plant* are sufficient to identify it. It is a plant worth knowing, for many consider it one of the most delicious of all edible fungi.

Edible but to be avoided: LEPIOTA RACHODES. *Poisonous but not fatal:* LEPIOTA MORGANI

These two species are so closely related and so much alike that we may consider them together. The chief reason for discussing them is that though both are fairly common one is edible and the other dangerously poisonous. If a person who claims to have some simple, infallible method for distinguishing edible mushrooms from poisonous ones could be given a basket of young or half-

Figure 29. *Lepiota morgani*, young plant. Poisonous but not fatal.

grown specimens of these two species mixed together and then be asked to pick out the good ones and eat them, it is likely that he would soon realize painfully how unreliable are his rules.

Lepiota morgani (Figures 29 and 30 and Plate 3C) usually comes up in the spring. The *spores*, in a spore print on white paper, *are pale green*, and the *gills of a mature plant are also pale green*, but *those of young, partly expanded specimens are white*. L. *rachodes*, on the other hand (Figures 31 and 32 and Plate 3D) usually comes

Figure 30. *Lepiota morgani*, green gills. Poisonous but not fatal.

up in the fall. The *spore print is white, the gills of young plants are white*, and they remain so or become pale tan in old specimens. The two species grow in similar locations, especially pastures and other grassy places, sometimes in fairy rings. Sometimes both come up at the same time, even intermingled with one another. They can be identified with certainty only by making a spore print, and this means making a sport print of *each specimen!*

Severe cases of poisoning by L. *morgani* are not uncommon, and since even people who consider themselves rather expert amateur

Figures 31 and 32. *Lepiota rachodes*. Edible but to be avoided.

mycologists have confused the two kinds and have been poisoned as a result, common sense directs us to avoid both species.

The caps are from 4 to 12 inches wide, those the size of a dinner plate and weighing more than a pound being not at all rare in a good season. In young plants the cap is spherical, with the margin attached to the stem, but later it becomes convex and finally almost flat. The surface of young specimens is nearly smooth or coarsely fibrous, and as the cap expands the fibrous outer layer cracks into large and prominent brown or white scales. The gills, free from the stem, are white when young. Those of the mature *Lepiota morgani* assume the pale green color of the spores; those of *Lepiota rachodes* remain white or turn a dingy tan. The stem is 1/2 to 1 1/2 inches thick at the top, increasing in diameter toward the base, where it is enlarged into a spherical bulb. It is from 4 to 10 inches long, its length seldom exceeding the diameter of the cap, and it bears a prominent ring above the middle. Fairy rings of *L. morgani* more than fifty feet across have been found, made up of dozens of specimens, each nearly a foot in diameter.

GENUS Marasmius

Edible and delectable: MARASMIUS OREADES (Fairy-ring Mushroom)

Marasmius means withered or shriveled, and the name was applied to this genus because, unlike most mushrooms, these plants wither in dry weather but do not die, and when moistened they revive, regain their original size and shape and freshness, and continue to shed spores. *Collybia confluens* also has this habit, as Figure 18 shows. This ability is of some benefit to them in that it enables them to survive periods of drouth that kill most other species. The specific name *oreades* means mountain nymphs, a poetical allusion to the fairy rings they form (Figures 33 and 34 and Plate 4A). Many kinds of mushrooms form such rings, but *Marasmius oreades* does so commonly. On pages 6–7 you may read how and why these rings develop.

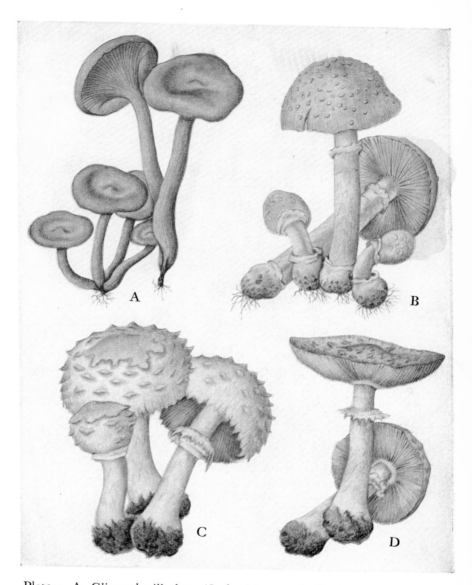

Plate 3. A. *Clitocybe illudens* (Jack-o'-Lantern). B. *Amanita russuloides*. C. *Lepiota morgani*. D. *Lepiota rachodes*. All poisonous except D.

Figures 33 and 34. *Marasmius oreades* (Fairy-ring Mushroom)
growing in a fairy ring. Edible and delectable.

The young plants are already formed when they first appear above the ground, but the caps are so small that they are scarcely visible. The caps of mature specimens are from 1/2 inch to 2 inches wide, ivory-colored or tan, smooth, with their rounded centers raised above the margins. The flesh is firm and white. The gills are white and far apart. The stems are from 2 to 4 inches long, slender but tough.

This species springs up everywhere in grassy lawns, fields, and orchards, literally thousands of them appearing in partial or complete rings. After one has located a few large rings he can be certain of a good supply of the mushrooms because several crops are borne each year, from spring until fall, and they continue to come up in the same place from year to year as long as the soil is left undisturbed. Insects seldom invade them, so even if the caps are withered and shrunk they are still perfectly good to eat, although if moist weather continues after a plant matures it may eventually decay and thus become inedible.

Fresh specimens can be dried in the sun or in a dry room and kept in this way indefinitely, needing only to be soaked in water half an hour before cooking to be as good as new. They are not at all tough, and the flavor is excellent. The recognition of this small but delectable and common fungus should be a "must" for those who are interested in eating wild mushrooms.

GENUS Panus

Edible but tough: PANUS RUDIS

This plant (Figure 35, page 64) is related to Lentinus and has the same leathery toughness but not to so great a degree. The cap is merely an extension of one side of the stem, and its surface is covered with a *dense reddish fuzz* that fades to tan in weathered specimens. The *gills are pale tan* and run down almost to the base of the stem. These are *comparatively small* mushrooms, being at the most 2 inches wide, but they *arise in clumps* that sometimes contain dozens of specimens, and it is not uncommon to see the sides of old dead trees and rotten stumps almost covered with them.

They are not injured by drying and will remain on a tree for weeks in perfectly good condition unless invaded by beetles. Because of their toughness they are more suitable for flavoring gravies and similar dishes than for solo consumption.

GENUS Pleurotus

Translated literally, the word Pleurotus means side ear, a term apt enough because some of the kinds included in this genus are more or less ear-like in shape and are attached to the wood from which they grow by means of a lateral, or side, stem. The genus is supposed to be recognized by (1) the white spores, (2) the stem attached at the side of the cap, or at least off center, and (3) the fleshy or tough texture of the cap, but actually there are no certain marks by means of which one can know the genus. Two of the common edible species, however, can be recognized easily.

Eminently edible: PLEUROTUS OSTREATUS (Oyster Mushroom)

The cap of this fungus (Figure 37) resembles an oyster in shape, whence the name, but the resemblance goes no farther, although the oyster mushroom makes excellent eating. Since it usually grows in clumps weighing a pound or more, each including five to ten fruit bodies, it is a good mushroom to become acquainted with. The cap is *kidney- or oyster-shaped* when viewed from above, *with a short stem tapering downward from one side;* it may be from 3 to 6 or 8 inches wide, projecting 3 to 5 inches outward from the place of attachment and sloping downward from the margin to the stem. The upper side is white or ivory-colored and quite smooth. The gills are white, and the white flesh is soft and spongy.

The only complaints that might be made against this species

Figure 35. *Panus rudis*. Edible but tough. Figure 36. *Pleurotus ulmarius*, mature plant. Edible.

Figure 37. *Pleurotus ostreatus* (Oyster Mushroom). Eminently edible. Figure 38. *P. sapidus*. Edible.

are, first, that in moist weather it decays very quickly and, second, that a ubiquitous breed of small beetles seems to consider the mushroom its particular booty, hundreds of them crawling in among the gills and feeding on the spores with voracious appetites. A young, fresh, uninfested clump, however, is a good find. Often several groups occur simultaneously, and they can be found on the same stump or log for several years in succession. In some parts of Europe whenever mushroom hunters find a good crop of *Pleurotus ostreatus* on a stump they water the stump at intervals to induce the production of further crops. According to accounts in one of the German journals, it can be readily cultivated on freshly cut stumps in the forest.

Edible: PLEUROTUS SAPIDUS

This species (Figure 38) is identical with the foregoing, P. *ostreatus,* in all respects except that it has very *pale violet spores,* instead of white, but the color is so pale that a heavy spore print, on white paper, is necessary to detect it. For this reason many mycologists consider P. *sapidus* merely a variety of P. *ostreatus.*

Edible: PLEUROTUS ULMARIUS

The specific name means growing on elm, and there are few mushroom hunters who do not know this common fall inhabitant of our elm and box elder trees (Figures 36 and 39). It grows out of branch stubs and knotholes, sometimes high up in the tree, and it usually emerges in the fall after all the leaves have gone.

The cap is from 3 to 6 inches wide, at first almost hemispherical, later flat, the surface white and either smooth or covered with flat scales. The gills and flesh are white, and the flesh is thick and firm. The stem is from 1/2 to 1 inch in diameter and from 4 to 6 inches long, curved outward from the tree and attached to the center of the cap.

This is a durable plant, as it would have to be at the season it

Figure 39. *Pleurotus uimarius*, young plant. Edible.

chooses to fruit. Low temperatures at night and even frequent frosts discourage it but little, although it grows slowly, often requiring two weeks to attain maturity. It is somewhat difficult to collect, since it is almost always out of reach, but with a long pole to which a knife has been attached one can, in a good season, collect a basketful on nearly any city street where old elms are growing. One or more fruit bodies come out of the same branch stub every year for a long period. Undoubtedly this fungus causes a great deal of heart rot in our ornamental elms, making the trees susceptible to wind throw, but no one knows just how much damage it causes or whether it would be practicable, or even possible, to dig it out.

Rusty Brown Spore Print

Edible: PHOLIOTA ADIPOSA (Fatty Pholiota)

Any gilled fungus having (1) cinnamon brown or rusty brown spores and (2) a definite ring on the stem belongs to the genus Pholiota. *Adiposa* means fatty or sticky, and this species (Figure 40) was so named because in fresh young specimens the upper surface of the cap is very sticky. It grows in crowded clumps of sometimes fifty specimens. The cap is from 3 to 5 inches in diameter, gently rounded, and chrome-yellow with dark brown scales. The gills are at first pale yellow but become dark brown as soon as the spores are produced in quantity. Often a cap immediately below the gills of a specimen above it will also be colored dark brown by the deposit of spores.

The stems are necessarily curved, since they arise from old branch stubs and other openings on standing trees in the city or in the woods, growing outward and upward to permit the formation of caps parallel to the surface of the earth. It often grows rather late in the fall, when few other mushrooms are to be found in abundance. A clump is likely to appear in the same place for many years, usually in the fall but sometimes in the spring. It is found throughout the country where hardwood forests grow, and although it is more common in forested areas than in towns it is by no means a stranger in the latter, and may be found on many a tree no farther afield than the back yard.

Even though this species is not among the best of the edible mushrooms, it is well worth knowing. The bright yellow clusters of fruit bodies are fairly easy to see for some distance, especially when they are borne near the bases of standing trees, and a single large clump will easily suffice for a meal. It is sometimes recommended that these mushrooms be peeled before you eat them.

Figure 40. *Pholiota adiposa* (Fatty Pholiota). Edible.

Pink Spore Print

Edible: CLITOPILUS ABORTIVUS

Clitopilus can be recognized by (1) the pale pink color of the spore print and (2) the fact that the gills are attached to the stem, sometimes running a short way down it. It grows on the ground, never on wood. *Clitopilus abortivus* (Figure 41) is the only common species, having been so named because of its frequently abortive shape, this malformation being due to the growth of a parasitic mold. Specimens not attacked by the mold have normal caps from 2 to 5 inches wide, convex in shape or with the margins raised slightly above the center; they usually pass from the former stage to the latter as they mature. The flesh is white and firm; it has a definite odor, difficult to describe but suggesting freshly ground grain and being at the same time slightly sharp.

The gills run down the stem 1/8 inch or less, are close together, narrow, grayish when young and a pale, dusty rose when mature. The stems are from 3 to 4 inches long and 1/4 to 1/2 inch in diameter, solid and fibrous. They grow either singly or in clumps, normal and diseased specimens side by side. Those infected with the mold are variously aborted, looking more like irregular puffballs than gilled fungi, although sometimes the mushroom stem and cap are evident. Both the normal and malformed specimens are good to eat, coming up in summer and fall near or under hardwood trees.

GENUS Pluteus

Edible but not choice: PLUTEUS CERVINUS

Pluteus is distinguished by (1) pink spores, (2) gills that do not touch the stem, and (3) the fact that the stem and cap are separable. That is, if one takes the cap in one hand and grasps the

Figure 41. *Clitopilus abortivus*. Edible. Normal specimens in the center; abortive specimens on either side.

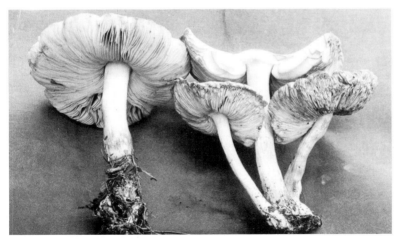

Figure 42. *Pluteus cervinus*. Edible but not choice.

71

stem with the other hand, pulling it gently from side to side, it will be detached easily from the flesh of the cap, leaving no torn shreds but only a smooth hemispherical or rounded hole. Although the spore color is officially pink, and in most species of the genus is definitely so, *Pluteus cervinus*, the most common species of the genus (Figure 42) makes an off-color spore print in which the pink is so diluted with tan that one might easily, on that basis alone, place it with the yellow-brown-spored group. However, it has gills that do not come within 1/8 inch of the stem, a definitely separable stem, and certain microscopic characters that make it a typical Pluteus.

The caps are shiny white to fawn-colored, from 4 to 6 inches wide, flat or gently sloping down from the center to the edge. The gills are so close together that when they lose their rigidity, with age, they collapse against one another; they are from 1/2 to 1 inch wide and, as stated above, do not touch the stem at all. The stem varies in length from 3 to 6 inches, in width from slender to stout, and is white and rather tough.

Several varieties of this common mushroom have been described, differing from each other chiefly in the color of the cap. It is fairly common in summer and fall, growing singly or in small groups on wood, sawdust, or compost.

Purple or Purple-Brown Spore Print

GENUS Agaricus

The edible qualities of members of this genus were known to the ancients, and it has the honor of being included in what was probably the first cookbook in the English language, written about 1390 by the chief cook of Richard II. One of the species described below, *Agaricus campestris,* is the principal cultivated mushroom of commerce. No one knows just when people learned that these mushrooms could be grown artificially, but the first record was made shortly after 1600, when the art was confined to a comparatively small area near Paris. Before World War I more than twenty miles of mushroom caves near Paris, mostly in abandoned stone mines, supplied much of Europe with fresh and canned mushrooms.

The "agarick" mentioned in some of the old herbals was not Agaricus but a woody bracket growing on coniferous trees and was erroneously supposed to be a specific cure for many of the ills to which our failing flesh is heir.

The name Psalliota is a synonym of Agaricus and is preferred by some botanists. It has the virtue of being more descriptive, since it is taken from the Greek word *psallion,* meaning a ring or collar, and refers to the ring surrounding the upper part of the stem. Agaricus is derived from a Greek word meaning mushroom and probably was merely one of several common terms used for fleshy fungi in general.

The genus is characterized by (1) the deep purple-brown spores, (2) the fleshy stem that can be separated easily from the cap, (3) the definite ring on the stem seen when the cap expands (this ring may wither and disappear later), and (4) gills free from the stem.

The young gills of most species are white before the cap opens, become pink as the spores begin to mature, and finally

73

turn almost black. The base of the stem is often slightly enlarged or bulbous, but it has no surrounding volva, or cup. Before the gills turn pink, Agaricus and deadly Amanita appear deceptively similar, but once the color of the spores is known there is no danger of confusing Agaricus with any of the poisonous mushrooms.

Several species of this genus are commonly found on lawns, in pastures, and in fields. All of them are equally good to eat, being among the best of the edible fungi.

Edible and choice: AGARICUS ABRUPTIBULBA

Figure 43. *Agaricus abrupti-bulba.* Edible and choice.

This bulbous-stemmed Agaricus (see Figures 43 and 44) is a common woods mushroom in late summer and fall, appearing in scattered groups or partial fairy rings from July until September, generally in hardwood forests. The cap is large, from 5 to 8 inches in diameter, and the stem is from 6 to 8 inches long, tapering gracefully upward from a base enlarged to a spherical bulb. The surface of the cap is *silky white; when scratched with a finger nail or sharply bruised it turns yellow.* This feature and the *large size* and the *bulbous base of the stem* constitute the identifying characteristics of *A. abruptibulba.*

The gills, white when the cap first opens, soon turn pink, then purple-brown. The ring on the stem of young specimens is very conspicuous, as can be seen in the illustration, but later disappears. This is an excellent mushroom for eating because of its

74

Figure 44. *Agaricus abruptibulba*. Edible and choice.

generous size and the added fact that several or many often come up near one another.

Eminently edible: AGARICUS CAMPESTRIS (Field Mushroom)

This is the common cultivated mushroom (Figure 45 and Plate 1C). In nature it is found scattered or in groups, sometimes in fairy rings or partial rings, on open, grassy ground, and it is by no means uncommon in and around cities.

When the caps first push up through the ground after a rain they are nearly spherical, like the button mushrooms sold in the markets. In a matter of hours, however, the caps expand and enlarge. In the button stage a layer of mycelium extends from the margin of the cap to the stem, protecting the gills, as in all species of Agaricus, but as the margin stretches out this veil is broken and forms the familiar, flaring ring on the stem. The *gills have*

75

Figure 45. *Agaricus campestris* (Field Mushroom).
Eminently edible.

Figure 46. *Agaricus rodmani* (Rodman's Mushroom). Eminently
edible. Note the characteristic ring on the stem.

almost always begun to turn pink by the time the veil has broken, and this gill color, combined with the *ring on the stem* and the *free gills,* makes the identification of it as a species of Agaricus almost foolproof. The cap is from 2 to 5 inches wide, the stem 1/2 to 1 inch thick and 2 to 5 inches long, usually rather short and squat. The flesh has an excellent flavor and is fairly tender, although some of the other species of Agaricus are considered better for eating.

Eminently edible: AGARICUS RODMANI (Rodman's Mushroom)

This mushroom (Figure 46) resembles *Agaricus campestris,* differing from it chiefly in its short, thick stem, its thick flesh and narrow gills, and the wide or double ring on the stem. The width of the gills *scarcely exceeds one third the thickness of the flesh of the cap,* a characteristic peculiar to this species. Also the wide or double ring is located below the middle of the stem; no other species of Agaricus has such a low waistline!

As in *A. campestris,* the gills do not touch the stem, and the color of the gills changes from white in very young plants to pink, and then to a dark purple-brown.

The cap normally expands while still an inch or two beneath the surface of the soil and is lifted up as the stem elongates, carrying a clump of earth above it. In size this mushroom resembles the preceding species, and as far as edibility is concerned the two could be considered identical. It is a common occupant of cities, and is found growing on lawns and along the grassy borders of streets.

GENUS Hypholoma

This genus has (1) violet to dark purple-brown spores, (2) a thin veil that breaks at the stem, leaving short-lived fragments of it clinging to the expanding cap, and (3) gills attached to the stem.

Figure 47. *Hypholoma incertum* (Uncertain Hypholoma). Edible but uninteresting. The veil has remained as a partial ring on the stem.

Edible but uninteresting: HYPHOLOMA INCERTUM
(Uncertain Hypholoma)

The name refers to the variability of this common mushroom (Figure 47 and Plate 4E). The cap is from 2 to 3 inches wide, convex or flat, at first pale tan but later white or nearly so. Sometimes inconspicuous silky scales are present on the surface. Delicate fragments of the veil remain attached to the margin of the cap for a short time before they dry up. As the cap opens, the gills are white, soon becoming a pale, then a dark, purple, their lower edges delicately fringed with white. The stems are slender, hollow, and brittle.

The plant grows in scattered groups around stumps and above woody debris buried in the soil, coming up from spring until fall. Successive crops may appear in the same place every year, or even several times a year for long periods. Though edible it is only average in flavor.

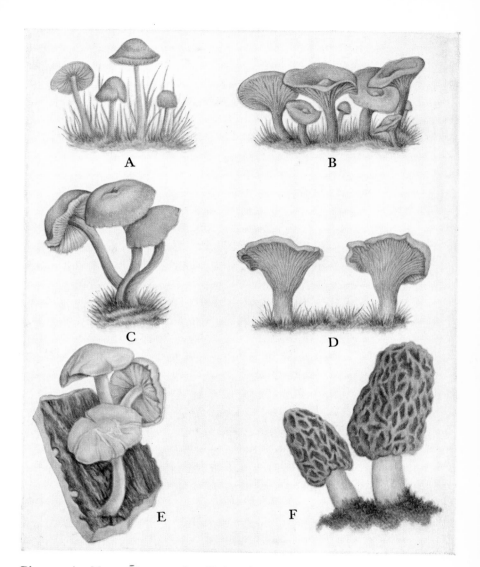

Plate 4. A. *Marasmius oreades* (Fairy-ring Mushroom). B. *Lactarius subdulcis*. C. *Clitocybe laccata*. D. *Cantharellus cibarius*. E. *Hypholoma incertum* (Uncertain Hypholoma). F. *Morchella crassipes* (Morel). All edible.

Figure 48. *Hypholoma sublateritium* (Brick-red Hypholoma). Edible.

Edible: HYPHOLOMA SUBLATERITIUM (Brick-red Hypholoma)

The common name of this plant (Figure 48 and Plate 2B) is descriptive of the color of the cap, which is from 1 to 4 inches wide, convex, *reddish brown in the center, paler toward the margin.* The gills of young specimens are at first *pale gray,* but as the spores mature they become *grayish brown, then purple-brown.* The stem is from 2 to 5 inches long, slender and curved, the upper part pale and the lower portion colored reddish brown like the cap. The plant grows in *dense clumps around decaying stumps and tree roots.* It is likely to be common in the fall.

Black Spore Print

Some authors state that the generic name Coprinus is derived from a word meaning dung and that it refers to the habit of several species that grow almost exclusively upon dung. Thomas, however, in the *Field Book of Common Gilled Mushrooms* (see page 119) states that the word means filthy and probably refers to the transformation of the gills into a slimy liquid. The genus is characterized (1) by black spores and (2) by a unique method of liberating these spores. The gills are so close together that they almost touch, and it is doubtful if many spores could be liberated were it not for the fact that the gills liquefy; this seems to occur through a process of autodigestion, the fungus producing enzymes that digest the cells of the gills and cap. This liquefaction begins at the bottom edge of the gills and progresses upward, the cap widening out gradually and the gills separating slightly during the process. The spores mature and are liberated just ahead of the advancing zone of liquefaction and thus float away in the air, although many are found in the liquid also.

All the common large species of Coprinus are edible, being of good flavor and very delicate texture. (A word of caution, however: some people have become ill from eating Coprinus after taking only a small alcoholic drink.) Their only drawback is that they must be picked before they mature and used almost at once. Since after they once appear above the ground they mature in a few hours to a day, one must practically be on the spot when they come up. If they are kept for more than a few hours after picking, one has, instead of mushrooms, a watery black mess.

Eminently edible: COPRINUS ATRAMENTARIUS
(Inky Cap)

This species (Figure 49) is somewhat less common than the two following but is still found frequently enough to deserve inclusion here, especially since it is also of choice quality.

Figure 49. *Coprinus atramentarius* (Inky Cap). Eminently edible.
Figure 50. *C. micaceus* (Mica, or Inky, Cap). Eminently edible.

Figure 51. *Coprinus comatus* (Shaggymane). Delicious. The larger
one is shedding spores, and its cap is liquefying. Figure 52. Mature
plant that has shed its spores; little remains of the cap.

The cap is shaped much like the pointed end of a hen's egg and is about that size or a little larger, *gray* in color, with very delicate *parallel furrows running from the margin up toward the center*. The margin is usually *split or scalloped in several places*. The gills are from 1/4 to 1/3 inch wide, packed tightly together except in the region where they are liquefying. The stem is about 1/4 inch in diameter and from 2 to 3 inches long, white and brittle, sometimes with a very narrow, inconspicuous ring where the margin of the cap was once attached.

This species grows on or near decayed wood, in dense clumps of half a dozen to fifty plants, so that if one finds it at all he is assured of enough for a good meal. Though generally found in hardwood forests and thickets, it is no stranger to lawns or gardens.

Delicious: COPRINUS COMATUS (Shaggymane)

This large and meaty mushroom is one of the best and most easily recognized of the common edible kinds (see "The Foolproof Four"; Figures 5, 51, and 52; Plate 1B). The cap is at first nearly cylindrical, from 1 1/2 to 2 inches wide and 4 to 6 inches high, covered with the *soft, shaggy scales* that suggested the common name. The gills are from 1/4 to 1/2 inch wide and are packed together solidly. Unless one gets very young specimens the lower edges of the gills will have begun to turn dark, but this portion can be cut off and discarded. The stem is white, about 1/2 inch thick, from 5 to 8 inches long, and rather fibrous and brittle. It grows on lawns, in parks, and in other grassy places from spring until fall. Usually several specimens appear near one another or grow tightly clumped together.

Eminently edible: COPRINUS MICACEUS (Mica Cap or Inky Cap)

This common small Coprinus (Figure 50 and Plate 1A) comes up in profusion around trees and stumps, apparently living chiefly on the decaying wood of the roots, and it is not uncommon for six or eight successive crops to appear each summer for several years. At Geneva, New York, a mycologist harvested ten crops from one elm stump during the spring and summer, some of these being induced to appear by watering the soil around the stump in periods of dry weather. The total weight of these ten crops was slightly more than thirty-eight pounds. Some maintain that this fungus can anticipate rain and will start to grow a day or two before the rain comes, doubtless because of the high humidity at that time.

The cap is at first conical, from 1 to 2 inches wide at the base, tan in moist weather but becoming nearly white when dried out, sometimes covered with exceedingly *small, shiny particles* and *marked with furrows* running from the margin up almost to the center. The gills are between 1/8 and 1/4 inch wide. The stem is about 1/8 inch wide and 2 or 3 inches long and is white and brittle.

It has been suggested that the spores of this and certain other fungi might be added to ink used in signing important documents, since a microscopic examination of the dried ink would reveal its identity and forgery would be unlikely, unless the forger was also a mycologist! This fungus, as well as all other species of Coprinus, is said to be digested more easily than most other kinds of mushrooms, since it is almost completely liquefied by its own enzymes, but it could scarcely be considered a sustaining food.

GENUS Panaeolus

Edible but not recommended: PANAEOLUS SOLIDIPES

The genus Panaeolus is known by (1) black spores and (2) gills that do not liquefy, as they do in Coprinus. This species (Figures 53 and 54) is the only one of sufficient size and prevalence to justify inclusion here. It is a spring mushroom com-

Figure 53. *Panaeolus solidipes*. Edible but not recommended.

mon on manured ground and on compost heaps containing straw and manure.

The cap is from 2 to 4 inches wide, hemispherical when young but later only somewhat convex, white or very pale yellow, and usually quite smooth. The gills are gray when young, becoming a variegated black and gray as they mature; in old specimens they are somewhat soft and slimy. The stem is from 4 to 6 inches long and seldom more than 1/4 inch wide, white, solid, and brittle. The top of the stem is *delicately ridged*, and *in young plants small droplets of liquid are exuded* from that portion just below the gills, *standing out in tiny clear beads*, as Figure 53 shows.

Figure 54. *Panaeolus solidipes*. Edible but not recommended.

84

Mushrooms without Gills

Puffballs

Anyone who has kicked a ripe puffball and has seen the cloud of powdery dust it shoots out knows why it was given this name, but not everyone knows that the little puff of powder contains millions of spores that serve to disseminate the fungus over the surface of the earth. The curiosity of man, which leads him to pick up such plants — perhaps even his anger at seeing an unknown plant, which leads him to destroy it with a kick — doubtless aids the humble puffball in liberating its spores. The tops of some puffballs crumble away at maturity, allowing the wind to spread the spores. Other kinds have only a pore at the top through which the spores escape, the force of even a gentle raindrop on the outside covering being enough to send out a million spores or so. In anything but a downpour these spores will travel some distance before being washed out of the air. Obviously there is a tremendous waste of spores, since the fungus depends upon the whims of the wind, and out of the billions of spores produced by a fair-sized specimen probably only a very few ever find a suitable place to grow.

Before the days of modern medicine, puffball spores were used as a styptic powder to stop bleeding, and even today in some places they are thought to be effective in the treatment of certain disorders. Children often believe that if puffball spores get into the eyes they will cause blindness, but this of course is pure superstition.

All the above-ground puffballs are good to eat, and they are believed by many to be superior to any other edible fungi (see "The Foolproof Four"). They must be picked while still solid and white inside and should be examined fairly carefully for the presence of maggots. The pear-shaped puffball, *Lycoperdon pyriforme* (Figure 2, page 20), is found in groups on rotten wood, and though small is of excellent flavor.

GENUS Calvatia

Edible and delicious: CALVATIA MAXIMA
(Giant Puffball)

This is undoubtedly one of the largest of all the fungi and at times it attains an almost unbelievable size. Schweinitz, one of the first American students of fungi, said about a hundred years ago that this puffball would reach a diameter of 3 feet. Specimens as large as a foot in diameter are common, and a specimen found in Minnesota several years ago was more than 2 feet high and weighed forty-five pounds. It has been estimated that a fairly large one would contain approximately eighteen billion spores.

This plant is seldom abundant, but it is not rare; some are found every year, occasionally in groups of five to ten or even more, in meadows, pastures, or woods during summer and fall. When sliced and fried it has few equals, but like all puffballs it is good to eat only as long as it is white and solid inside. The fruit bodies are nearly spherical, or else somewhat greater in height than in diameter, white and smooth when young, becoming tan or brown at maturity, when the upper part of the wall collapses to allow the spores to escape.

Edible and choice: CALVATIA CAELATA (Carved Puffball); C. CYATHIFORMIS (Vase-shaped Puffball)

These two species are probably more common than *C. maxima*, being found in some abundance every year in pastures and open fields (Figures 2 and 3). They look very much alike, averaging from 4 to 6 inches in diameter and slightly more than that in height, with a white, warty surface. Usually the upper part is nearly spherical but narrows downward to a thick, stem-like base. The upper part of the wall crumbles away at maturity, leaving a cup-shaped structure filled with spores. The mature spores of *C. caelata* are chocolate brown in color, and those of *C. cyathi-*

88

formis are a deep purple-brown, this being the chief distinguishing feature between them.

Both species are good to eat, of delicate, crumbly texture and delicious flavor. If one finds any at all he is likely to find several, because they grow in scattered colonies, and this habit and their excellent flavor make them well worth knowing.

GENUS Scleroderma

Poisonous: SCLERODERMA VULGARE

This puffball is not at all rare in some wooded regions but is seldom found because it usually grows an inch or more beneath the surface of the ground and is exposed only by erosion, the burrowing of animals, or, more often, the rooting of pigs. Sometimes, however, it does push up above the surface at maturity. It is said to be poisonous, and evidence in support of this fact was obtained by a man who some years ago had found some and asked a professional mycologist about their edibility. He was told that they were suspected of being poisonous and should not be eaten. Two weeks later he called again, to inform the mycologist that he was certain they were poisonous because he had eaten some and consequently had been in the hospital for a week!

The fruit bodies are nearly spherical, about the size of a golf ball, white or pale yellow at first, but later leathery brown. A dense clump of root-like mycelium is usually attached to the base. The wall is strong and leathery, about 1/8 inch thick, much thicker than that of other puffballs, and the spore mass is almost black. The *thick wall* and *dark purple or black interior of even young specimens* make it so easy to recognize that there is no danger of confusing it with the edible puffballs that grow on the surface of the ground.

Morels and Saddle Fungi

Edible and unexcelled: GENUS Morchella

There can scarcely be any doubt that the morels (see "The Foolproof Four," Figure 1, and Plate 4F) are practically without equals as edible fungi, and in regions where they are common they are sought avidly by mushroom enthusiasts. In flavor and texture they surpass both the common cultivated species and most other wild mushrooms, and attempts have been and still are being made to grow them commercially — so far without success. Anyone who succeeded would have a veritable gold mine if he could keep his secret and avoid glutting the market, because morels command a good price and always are in demand.

One year they will be found in abundance on certain hillsides, but they may not reappear there for years. They seem to come up readily in some burned-over areas, and it is said that at one time the residents of some parts of Germany made such a practice of burning the woodlands to encourage the growth of morels that they had to be restrained by law. Morels are fairly common in some wooded areas throughout what was known as the Big Woods in early Minnesota days, as well as in the Central States and the East, but if sought at the right time they can be found in abundance in almost every state of the Union.

They appear for a short time only, usually in the early spring, the season in the northern United States being at its peak during May. There are several species, but they are all enough alike to be described as one. The cap is conical, from 3 to 4 inches high and from 1 to 2 inches wide at the base. The surface is tan and is indented with large, irregular pits or cavities, so that the plant resembles an animal sponge. The stem is white and very delicate and brittle in texture, breaking readily when handled, and averages about 1 inch in thickness and 2 or 3 inches in length. Both stem and cap are hollow.

These fungi are especially recommended for eating because no one who has seen even a picture of a morel could confuse the plants with any poisonous kinds. They are absolutely safe for any amateur to collect and eat and, moreover, are exceedingly delicious. When one finds a spot where morels grow thickly it is well to keep it a secret, since one's friends will have no compunction about arriving first at the harvest.

GENUS Helvella

Edible: HELVELLA CRISPA

Species of Helvella are known as the saddle fungi because of the marked resemblance of the caps to the shape of a saddle. Several kinds are found; the most common is *Helvella crispa* (Figure 55), the species name meaning wavy and referring to the margin of the cap. They grow singly or in groups of two, three, or four in wooded regions and swamps and can be found rather readily because of their pure white color. The cap is *more or less irregularly saddle-shaped* and varies in width up to 2 inches; the stem is most marvelously *fluted and twisted.*

No other species resembles this one closely enough to be mistaken for it.

GENUS Gyromitra

Edibility doubtful: GYROMITRA ESCULENTA

This mushroom is closely related to the saddle fungi and therefore may be considered in the same group. Gyromitra means gyrose or convoluted and refers to the characteristic shape of the cap, which is made up of rounded folds (Figure 56). This is one of the more common spring mushrooms in wooded areas; it often grows in low places and swamps but is by no means restricted to sites of that kind. The cap is *chocolate brown,* up to 4 or 5 inches in diameter, much *ridged and convoluted, brittle, and hollow.* The stem is *short, thick, white,* and sometimes branched at the top.

Figure 55. *Helvella crispa*. Edible.

The species name, *esculenta*, refers to the excellent edibility of the fungus, but there is abundant reason to question the wisdom of partaking too freely, or even at all, of this fungus. Granted that many people have eaten it in quantity and for years and have only the highest admiration for its quality, the fact remains that in both Europe and America it has been known with certainty to have caused fatal poisoning. Many of these cases have been too well authenticated to permit reasonable doubt as to the identity of the fungus responsible. Such

Figure 56. *Gyromitra esculenta*. Edibility doubtful.

cases are rare, to be sure, and most of them have occurred among people who were sick or undernourished. Considering the extent to which the fungus is eaten and the general excellence of its reputation, it is with some misgivings that the author puts it on his blacklist, but the fact that it has been known, unquestionably, to poison people is sufficient justification for condemning it.

Pore Fungi

Edible: POLYPORUS SULPHUREUS (Sulphur Shelf Mushroom, or Sulphur Polypore)

This colorful fungus has been described and illustrated (Figure 4) in "The Foolproof Four" section in sufficient detail so that it need not be discussed here.

GENUS Strobilomyces

Edible: STROBILOMYCES STROBILACEUS
(Cone Fungus)

Figure 57. *Strobilomyces strobilaceus* (Cone Fungus). Edible.

The common name of this fungus is suggested by the resemblance of the tufts on the cap to scales on pine cones (Figure 57). In the young plant the cap is spherical and covered with a *thick layer of woolly, dark mycelium* that breaks up into soft, pyramidal tufts as the cap expands, exposing a paler brown layer beneath. In maturity the cap is convex or flat and from 3 to 5 inches wide. The flesh of the cap is from 1/4 to 1/2 inch thick near the stem, thin at the margin, soft and dry, pale tan when first broken, soon becoming reddish brown and often exuding a reddish-brown juice. After the flesh has been exposed to the air for some minutes, it becomes dark blue.

94

The pores on the under side of the cap are dark brown, soft, and from 1/3 to 1 inch long. The stem is firm, from 3 to 6 inches long, less woolly than the cap. A newly expanded specimen will have a ring near the upper part of the stem, but this soon withers and disappears.

This fungus is common during the summer and fall, usually growing in groups on the ground in wooded areas. Its edibility is good, and it cannot be confused with any other fungus. Because of its naturally soft texture and dark interior, decay or the presence of maggots is less obvious than in many other fungi, and one must be careful to select only fresh, sound specimens for eating.

GENUS Fistulina

Eminently edible: FISTULINA HEPATICA (Beefsteak Fungus)

Since this mushroom is not common in the North Central States the author has been unable to study it at first hand, but in the East, where it is common on the trunks and stumps of living or dead trees, it is unmistakable and of desirable edibility. The plants grow out horizontally from the tree. The cap is *blood-red* when fresh, *liver-shaped*, with a *wavy or scalloped margin*. The flesh of the cap is soft, thick, and juicy, and the pores on the under side are yellowish. A short, lateral stem is sometimes present.

Club Fungi

Edible: GENUS Clavaria

All Clavarias are edible, and although the texture of most of them is definitely tough, the flavor is usually excellent, and they lend themselves readily to drying. There are many different spe-

Figure 58. *Clavaria stricta.* Edible.

cies, some of them too small to deserve notice for our purposes, but others large, conspicuous, easily recognized, and common. The photograph of *Clavaria stricta* growing on a rotten aspen log (Figure 58) shows the general Clavaria form and habit better than words. Characteristic are (1) their upright growth and (2) their repeatedly branching stems, the tips of which always point upward. The number of branches in a clump varies from a few dozen to several hundred, and a large fruit body will be 5 or 6 inches across and 3 or 4 inches high. The color varies from pale tan to brown or ashy gray. They grow on old decayed logs and stumps and on the ground around dead trees and can be found in abundance throughout the wooded areas of most of the North Temperate Zone. It is entirely probable that some species have better culinary qualities than have been attributed to them in the past and that if given a fair trial by those willing to experiment with methods of preparation they would acquire an excellent reputation as edible fungi.

Should any reader be interested in learning more about this group he is referred to Coker's extensive monograph on Clavaria- ceae (listed in the Bibliography on page 119), wherein a large number of species are described and illustrated, many of them in color.

Tooth Fungi

GENUS Hydnum

These are less common and abundant than the club fungi, to which they are related, but some of them are encountered often enough to merit inclusion here. The two species illustrated (Figures 59 and 60) are so characteristic that they cannot be confused with other kinds and for this reason should be of interest and value to the beginner.

Edible: HYDNUM CAPUT-URSI (Bear's Head Fungus)

Figure 59. *Hydnum caput-ursi* (Bear's Head Fungus). Edible.

The bear's head fungus forms white clumps from 3 to 6 inches or more in diameter, made up of *hundreds of tapering teeth,* each tooth being from 2 to 4 inches long.

We have found only a few of these rarely beautiful plants, but in some years and in some places they are fairly common, inhabiting hardwood forests throughout most of the United States. This species probably causes some decay in living trees (the photographed specimen was found on a felled oak tree, but its beauty and edibility atone for any damage it may do.

Edible: HYDNUM CORALLOIDES (Coral Fungus)

The coral fungus grows as hemispherical clumps that may be a foot across but are ordinarily from 4 to 8 inches wide. The fruit body originates from a single stem, which branches repeatedly.

Figure 60. *Hydnum coralloides* (Coral Fungus). Edible.

All the branches bear *short, awl-shaped teeth that point down-ward*, as in the rest of the genus.

This species is found only on decayed hardwood logs but is not at all uncommon. Because of its size and pure white color it can often be recognized at a distance and, since a single fruit body may weigh a pound or more, one does not have to find many to suffice for a meal.

Both of these fungi can probably be ranked as only average in edibility. Their flavor is attractive enough, but it tends to be rather bland, and the texture is somewhat tough. One point in their favor, however, is that they are seldom inhabited by insects.

Jelly Fungi

The jelly fungi are so named because many of them have the appearance of irregular lumps of jelly and because the texture of fresh specimens is definitely gelatinous. All of them, however, are edible. People familiar with wooded areas will almost certainly have seen various jelly fungi, especially the two widely distributed and easily recognized kinds here described.

GENUS Hirneola

Edible: HIRNEOLA AURICULA-JUDAE (Jew's Ear Fungus)

The Jew's ear (Figure 61) is a cosmopolitan plant found almost throughout the world. The cap is from 1 to 2 inches across, typically *ear-shaped, dark brown* in color, and attached by a lateral or off-center stem-like base. It usually grows in colonies on coniferous and hardwood logs for several years after the trees have fallen, and it can often be gathered in quantity. In texture it is somewhat tough-gelatinous and in flavor rather bland. It can be dried easily and kept indefinitely, needing only to be soaked in water for a short time before being used.

One kind of Jew's ear is cultivated after a fashion, on wood cut for the purpose, in at least one region of China and is exported to other sections of that country. There it is highly esteemed as food and is considered to have various medicinal virtues as well. Another species or variety occurs in great abundance in New Zealand and other islands of the South Pacific, and the gathering and exportation of it have been of some commercial importance. From 1872 to 1883, according to Cooke's *British Edible Fungi* (see page 119), 1,858 tons of Jew's ear fungi, valued at about eighty thousand pounds sterling, were exported from

Figure 61. *Hirneola auricula-judae* (Jew's Ear Fungus). Edible.
Figure 62. *Tremella lutescens* (Yellow Jelly Fungus). Edible.

New Zealand to the Orient. This should be a clinching argument for its edibility.

GENUS Tremella

Edible: TREMELLA LUTESCENS (Yellow Jelly Fungus)

This fungus (Figure 62) is a common inhabitant of old logs, where it grows as a convoluted, soft, gelatinous mass. It was once known as "witch's butter," from the fanciful belief that it was associated in some way with witches. It is edible but has never attained much favor in Europe or America, perhaps because the plant is small and tends to become slimy with age or perhaps because methods of preparing it to bring out its best qualities have not yet been devised.

Mushroom Cookery

Mushroom Cookery

The History of Mushroom Eating

Before you try the recipes for cooking mushrooms, you may be interested to know that they have been a highly prized and often considerable part of the diet of man in many lands and for many centuries. They are mentioned as food in the Talmud and in Chaldean writings that date from the dawn of civilization. More than twenty centuries ago the eating of fungi became a mania among the rich in Rome, and for a time the passion for mushrooms was synonymous with an unseemly and undisciplined love of luxuries. Special vessels were used to cook certain kinds, and a poet of the day makes one such vessel complain because it has fallen so low as to be used for cooking Brussels sprouts!

This remarkable taste for mushrooms was partly social affectation, to be sure, but it was based upon the sound fact that they are a palatable and delicious food. It is perhaps worthy of emphasis that no mushrooms were cultivated then or for a long time after that, and the widespread demand for edible fungi was necessarily satisfied by those collected in the wild.

The Romans had rules of thumb by means of which they recognized the edible kinds, and these rules probably worked fairly well most of the time. They were, however, unreliable in so far as they disregarded real distinguishing characteristics, and they were often interwoven with superstition. One of the fireside naturalists of the time stated that those mushrooms growing near serpent holes or rusty nails were sure to be poisonous, but there is no reason to suppose that those "in the know" put much stock in such ideas. At that time most practical knowledge of plants consisted of folklore, and the real authorities on mushroom eating were those who learned to know their mushrooms through experience and observation. To a certain extent this still holds true, and many an authority on mushrooms retains an unclouded amateur status.

One finds little mention of mushrooms from the time of the Romans up to the last century. The *Grete Herball,* published about 1529, an authoritative if often inaccurate treatise on plants, contents itself with stating, "Fungi ben musherons. There be two maners of them, one maner is deadly and sleeth them that eateth of them and the other dooth not" — a statement that even the most illiterate faggot-cutter in the forest must have known from experience to be only partially true. Caspar Bauhin, eminent Swiss botanist of the same century and considered one of the fathers of modern botany, damns all mushrooms, obviously because he knew them only from hearsay. The professional botanists disliked fungi of any kind because they found these plants difficult or impossible to classify in their artificial keys, and consigned them to chaos or worse. But people continued to eat them nevertheless!

Up to the present time (at least until the outbreak of World War II) in many of the countries of Europe the quantity of wild mushrooms offered for sale in the public markets has far exceeded that of the one or two cultivated kinds, and in India and China the traffic in wild mushrooms has always been heavy.

It is hoped that this brief summary will convince even the most skeptical that mushroom eating has never been confined to one region or time, that it does not partake of the strange or the esoteric but rather is a common pleasure, open to all. The first recipe in the next section, indeed, is three hundred years old — and quite as good today as it was when it was first written down.

General Recipes for Cooking Wild Mushrooms

The famous old recipe for jugged hare reads, "First catch your hare." So far in this book we have been busy helping you to catch your mushrooms and to be sure they are the ones that you can safely eat. Now you will find recipes for cooking the mushrooms you have caught. The choice of recipe will depend, of course, on the kind and quantity of your catch.

Unless there is some obvious reason for doing so, mushrooms need not be peeled, nor do the gills have to be removed. Wipe them clean with a damp cloth and cut off the ends of the stems after you have inspected them according to the directions for gathering mushrooms on pages 14–16. Soaking them in water impairs the flavor and is unnecessary.

"According to the views of many persons," says a government bulletin * on wild mushrooms, "mushrooms are best cooked simply, with no seasoning but butter, pepper, and salt. The addition of various seasonings impairs the delicate mushroom flavor. Mushrooms may be prepared for the table in any way which would be suitable for oysters." This is an interesting observation that amateur mushroom collectors may wish to put to the test in their own kitchens.

While mushrooms are eaten principally for their excellent flavor, recent evidence indicates that they are a wholesome and nourishing food as well. The common cultivated mushroom contains nearly 4 per cent protein, more copper and iron in assimilable form than most other common foods, and relatively large quantities of riboflavin and nicotinic acid. In general cultivated mushrooms offer about as much nourishment as some of the common fruits and vegetables. The available data suggest that a number of wild mushrooms have a somewhat similar food value.

"TO DRESS A DISH OF FUNGEE" †

"Take them fresh gathered and putt them betweene two dishes, and sett them on a Chaifing Dish of Coles, and there lett them Stewe, and putt nothing to them in the first Stewing for they will Yeald Liquor enough of them selves, and When all the Water is stewed out of them, power that Liquor Cleane from them and putt a good quantitye of Sallitt Oyle unto them and Stewe them

---

* Flora W. Patterson and Vera K. Charles. *Some Common Edible and Poisonous Mushrooms.* U. S. Department of Agriculture, Farmers' Bulletin No. 796 (Washington: Government Printing Office. 1922).

† A seventeenth-century recipe.

therein. Wringe in the joyce of one or two Lemmons, or else putt in some Vinniger and putt in a little Nuttmegg and two or three Blades of Mace.

"If your Lord or Lady Loves not Oyle, Stewe them with a Little Sweete Butter and a little White Wine."

MUSHROOM SOUP 1 *

Take 1 quart of any edible mushrooms, carefully cleaned. Put in a covered pan with 3 pints of water, and boil slowly for one hour. Rub the whole through a colander. Reject whatever does not rub through readily. Add 1/2 pint of milk thickened with 1 tablespoonful of flour, 1 ounce of butter, 1 dessertspoonful of salt, and 1 teaspoonful of pepper. Bring to a boil, then serve. Other vegetables, such as celery, can of course be added to increase the nutritive value.

MUSHROOM SOUP 2 †

Sauté the caps gently in butter until they are cooked through but not browned. Put the stems through a medium fine grinder, being careful to save the juice and return it to the ground mushrooms. Slice the cooked caps thinly or put them through the grinder, whichever you prefer.

For 1 pound of mushrooms, put 1 quart of rich top milk or half cream and half whole milk into a double boiler. Add a green onion or a slice of a mild dry onion and then the prepared mushrooms. Bring slowly to a simmer. Add 1 cup or more of strong chicken broth. With 1 teaspoonful of flour that has been cooked but not browned in the butter in which the mushroom caps were sautéed, thicken to the consistency of heavy cream. Remove the onion, season to taste, and let stand in the double boiler until served. Garnish with whipped cream dusted with paprika or with finely chopped parsley.

* From Charles McIlvaine and Robert K. MacAdam. *One Thousand American Fungi.* Indianapolis: Bobbs-Merrill Co. 1902, 1930. Quoted by special permission of the publisher.

† By courtesy of Mrs. Frances del Plaine, Minneapolis.

BAKED MUSHROOMS *

Wipe off the caps with a damp cloth, dip them in bread or cracker crumbs, place them in a pan with the gills up, add a small piece of butter to each, season with salt and pepper, cover tightly, and bake in a moderate oven for 20 to 30 minutes. If you have enough mushrooms, several layers, one on top of another, can be baked in this way. Serve on toast or corn bread.

CREAMED MUSHROOMS (MUSHROOM PÂTÉS) *

Cut the mushrooms into small pieces. Heat 2 ounces of butter to each pint of mushrooms, and when this begins to smoke drop the mushrooms in and cover them. Cook for 10 to 20 minutes, stirring occasionally to prevent burning. Remove the cover, draw the mushrooms to one side, and tilt the pan so that the juice runs to the other side. Into this work 1 tablespoonful of flour and, when smooth, add 1/2 pint of milk or cream. Stir the mushrooms into this and allow to boil for a minute. Season to taste, fill prepared pâté shells with them, heat for a few minutes in the oven, and serve. (These creamed mushrooms may also be served on toast.)

FRIED MUSHROOMS †

Beat the yolk of an egg with 1 tablespoonful of water and season with pepper and salt. Dip each cap in this and then dip into fine cracker crumbs or corn meal. Have butter or cooking oil very hot in a frying pan. Fry slowly on each side for 5 minutes. A sauce can be made by thickening with flour and adding milk or cream. A smooth tomato sauce is also excellent.

MUSHROOMS WITH BACON †

Fry as much bacon as you need, and on removing it from the frying pan keep it hot. Cook the mushrooms on each side in the "fryings" and serve on a platter with the strips of bacon arranged

* From M. E. Hard. *The Mushroom.* Columbus: Mushroom Publishing Co. 1908.
† From the U.S.D.A. Bull. No. 796.

as a border. Almost any small species are good prepared in this manner.

MUSHROOMS COOKED WITH CREAM UNDER A GLASS COVER OR BELL *

With a small biscuit cutter cut round slices of bread; they should be about 2 1/2 inches in diameter and about 1 inch in thickness. Cut the stems close to the gills from fresh mushrooms; wash and wipe the mushrooms. Heat 1 tablespoonful of butter in a saucepan; throw in the mushrooms, skin side down. Cook just a moment, and sprinkle with salt and pepper. After the rounds of bread have been slightly toasted, arrange them in the bottom of a bell dish and heap the mushrooms on them. Put a little piece of butter in the center; cover over with the bell, which may be of glass, china, or silver; stand them in a baking pan, and then place in the oven for 20 minutes. While these are cooking, mix 1 table-spoonful of butter and 1 tablespoonful of flour in a saucepan. Add either 1/2 pint of milk or 1/2 pint of half-and-half milk and chicken stock. Stir until it boils; then add 1/2 teaspoonful of salt and a dash of pepper. When the mushrooms have been in the oven the allotted time, take them out; lift the cover, pour over quickly a little of this sauce, cover again, and serve at once.

DEVILED MUSHROOMS *

Chop or break into small pieces 1 quart of mushrooms, season with pepper and salt; prepare 1 pint of bread crumbs; mix the mashed yolk of 2 hard-boiled eggs with 2 raw ones and stir into 1 cup of milk or cream. Put a layer of crumbs in the bottom of a baking pan or dish, then a layer of mushrooms; scatter over bits of butter; pour on a part of the cream and egg mixture, and continue until the dish is full, having bread crumbs with butter for the top layer. Bake for 20 minutes, closely covered, in a hot oven; then uncover for about 5 minutes, or long enough for the top to be well browned. If you prefer, water and lemon juice may be substituted for milk or cream.

* From the U.S.D.A. Bull. No. 796.

MUSHROOM COOKERY

MUSHROOMS BAKED WITH TOMATOES *

In a baking dish arrange small round slices of buttered toast; upon each piece place a rather thin slice of peeled tomato, salted and peppered. Upon each slice of tomato place a fine, thick mushroom, gill side up; in the center of each mushroom put a generous piece of butter. Season with pepper and salt. Cover the dish and bake in a hot oven for 10 minutes; then uncover and bake for an additional 5 to 10 minutes, as the mushrooms appear to require.

PEPPERS STUFFED WITH MUSHROOMS *

Cut the stem end of the peppers and carefully remove all seeds and the white membrane. Wash the mushrooms. Chop or break them into small pieces, season with pepper and salt, press firmly into the peppers, and put a good-sized lump of butter on top of each. The water adhering to the mushrooms after washing will furnish sufficient moisture for cooking.

Arrange the peppers on end in a baking dish, having the water with salt, pepper, and butter poured in to the depth of about 1 inch. Place the dish in a hot oven, cook covered for 15 minutes; then uncover and baste and cook for 10 or 15 minutes longer, or until the peppers are perfectly tender. An addition of chopped cooked chicken or veal to the mushrooms is a pleasing and nutritious variation.

MUSHROOM OMELET †

Prepare an omelet of 6 eggs, salt, pepper, and a dash of paprika. . . . Beat your eggs with a fork but not more than is necessary to mix the white and the yolk. Use a heavy iron skillet, place a generous amount of butter in it, and when it begins to brown, add your eggs and finish your omelet as usual. You will have prepared your mushrooms before this, however. A quarter pound, sliced, and lightly sautéed in butter. Pour over the omelet, fold, and serve at once.

* From the U.S.D.A. Bull. No. 796.
† Helmut Ripperger. *Mushroom Cookery*. New York: George W. Stewart. 1941.

COMMON EDIBLE MUSHROOMS

STUFFED EGGPLANT *

Parboil an eggplant for about 20 minutes. Split in half length-wise and remove the inside and chop it up. Take 1/4 pound of mushrooms and sauté them for a few minutes in butter, and, just before they are done, add some minced onion. Mix the mushrooms with the chopped eggplant and return into the two halves. Sprinkle lightly with bread crumbs, freshly grated Parmesan, and dab with a little soft butter. Bake in a moderate oven for 20 minutes.

MUSHROOM PURÉE *

Chop 1/2 pound of mushrooms and fry in 1 ounce of butter for a few minutes until they are done. Add 2 tablespoons of brown gravy and simmer for a few minutes more. Add salt, pepper, and the yolk of an egg. . . . Take the whites of 2 eggs . . . beat them stiff, and mix with the mushrooms. Butter some ramekins, fill with the mixture and bake in a moderate oven for 15 minutes.

MUSHROOM MOUSSE *

Cook 1/2 pound of mushrooms in salted water with a little lemon juice until they are done. Drain them well and chop them together with 4 ounces of lean boiled ham. Add 4 tablespoons of white sauce, salt and pepper. Soak 1/2 ounce of gelatine in a little cold water for 5 minutes. Add to the mixture and then let it cool. Whip 1/2 pint of cream and gradually fold in with the rest. Set on ice until firm.

STEWED CHINESE MUSHROOMS *

This is made with dried mushrooms. Soak 1/2 pound of mushrooms in warm water for an hour, drain, and rinse. Crush 2 cloves of garlic and cook for a few minutes in a pan brushed with oil. Remove the garlic. Put the mushrooms in the pan and cook for 15 minutes. Add enough stock to cover, a small piece of ginger shredded, bring to a boil and simmer for several hours. Serve with soy bean sauce.

*From H. Ripperger. *Mushroom Cookery.*

MUSHROOMS MARJORIE, WITH WILD RICE *

Remove stems from 1 pound of mushrooms. Place these in a pan and add 1 1/2 cups of meat stock or water, 1/2 teaspoon of salt, a dash of pepper, 1 small onion cut in quarters, 1 stalk of celery cut in pieces, a sliver of nutmeg, 2 bay leaves, and a small piece of stick cinnamon. Cover tightly, bring to a boil, and simmer for 1 hour. Strain off the stock, probably about 1 cup.

Melt 2 ounces of butter in a heavy skillet. Add 1 onion and 1 celery heart, both finely chopped. Sauté until soft but not brown. Add the mushrooms cut in slices 1/4 inch thick. Cover and cook 10 minutes. Then add 1/4 cup of flour and blend well; next pour in the 1 cup of stock strained from the stewed stems and also 1/2 cup of cream. Stir until thickened, cover, and cook very gently for 1/2 hour. Just before serving add 1/2 cup sour red wine, a dash of worcestershire sauce, and salt and pepper to taste; heat just to the boiling point and serve on fried wild rice, garnished with paprika.

To prepare fried wild rice: Wash carefully 3/4 cup of wild rice. Spread it out on clean absorbent paper for at least an hour. Heat deep fat until it just gives off a blue smoke; drop in the rice, about 1 tablespoonful at a time. As it rises to the top of the fat, skim off with a strainer. Keep very hot until ready to serve.

Recipes for Cooking Certain Species

Most species of wild mushrooms may be used in the preceding recipes, if they are not too tough or if they are not of unusual size, texture, or flavor. These qualities are mentioned in the descriptions of the various species. However, some kinds lend themselves to special methods of preparation. The following recipes will give you suggestions.

MUSHROOM SALADS †

For salads many mushrooms may be used raw, after being

* By courtesy of Mrs. John Reighard, Minneapolis.
† From the U.S.D.A. Bull. No. 796.

peeled, especially species of Coprinus and Clavaria and all puff-balls. Tougher plants can be stewed, drained, and chilled before adding the dressing, which may be either a mayonnaise or a French dressing of oil with vinegar or lemon juice. Serve on lettuce.

HONEY FUNGUS (ARMILLARIA MELLEA)*

This species is excellent when fried and served on toast. It is also good stewed.

FAIRY-RING MUSHROOMS (MARASMIUS OREADES)*

(1) Fairy-ring mushrooms are popular when stewed and served with a brown sauce as an accompaniment to beefsteak. Dried mushrooms may be revived by soaking in water.

(2) Pickles can be made after the fungi have been packed in jars. Pour over them highly spiced, scalding vinegar. Allow them to stand for at least 2 weeks.

ELM CAPS, OR OYSTER CAPS (PLEUROTUS ULMARIUS)

(1) Put into the pan beside a pork roast and cook for an hour or more. Season slightly when nearly done. †

(2) Take small specimens or cut from large, tender ones pieces the size of oysters. Dip in the beaten yolk of an egg to which 1 tablespoonful of water has been added and roll in cracker crumbs or corn meal. Season with salt and pepper. Fry in either deep fat, melted butter, or oil.*

INKY CAPS AND SHAGGYMANES (COPRINUS)*

The species of this genus are very delicate, *Coprinus micaceus* being considered the most easily digested of all mushrooms. They are good when steamed for 5 minutes and served with butter or cream.

Species of Coprinus are also delicious baked with cheese. Butter a baking dish and put in a layer of mushrooms, bread crumbs,

* From the U.S.D.A. Bull. No. 796.
† By courtesy of Mrs. Frances del Plaine, Minneapolis.

and cheese grated or cut into small pieces; season with pepper and salt. Repeat the process once or twice, according to the quantity to be prepared, adding a few small lumps of butter to the last layer. Bake for 15 or 20 minutes.

PUFFBALLS (CALVATIA)

(1) Peel and use raw in salad.*

(2) Slice and fry in butter. Or dip slices first in beaten egg and cracker crumbs, then fry. A cream dressing is a delicious addition to fried puffballs.*

(3) Cut in 1/2 inch slices and fry gently in butter until well heated but not browned. Mash fine with a fork, a wire potato masher, or a potato ricer. Season and add as much heavy cream as the mushrooms will absorb. Heat, then serve on thin buttered toast.†

(4) Dice the puffballs; stew for 15 minutes in a small quantity of water. Pour off the water; dust with a little flour; add a small quantity of milk or cream, butter, pepper, and salt, a little parsley, and a trace of powdered onion or garlic. Stew slowly for 5 minutes before serving.‡

MORELS (MORCHELLA) *

All morels are delicious. Probably the best manner of preparing them is simply to fry them lightly in butter. Another good way is to stuff them with chopped cooked chicken or veal, moistened bread or cracker crumbs and seasoned simply with salt and pepper. The stalks should be split to permit the stuffing and then tied together before the morels are baked. In the covered baking dish there should be a very small quantity of water. Bake until the morels are tender.

SULPHUR SHELF (POLYPORUS SULPHUREUS) †

The sulphur shelf is delicious sliced and fried in butter or

* From the U.S.D.A. Bull. No. 796.
† By courtesy of Mrs. Frances del Plaine.
‡ From C. McIlvaine and R. MacAdam. *One Thousand American Fungi.*

breaded and fried. This fungus greatly resembles the breast of chicken in flavor when so prepared, and is perfection itself.

BEEFSTEAK FUNGUS (FISTULINA HEPATICA) *

The beefsteak fungus should be sliced across the grain and soaked in salt water, the length of time varying with its age. The slice should be wiped dry and boiled or fried, then dressed with butter, salt, and pepper.

The fungus may be used raw for salad, dressed to suit the taste, stewed, or made into soup. The suggestion of its use as a foundation for a beefsteak pie is apparently worthy of experiment, as its resemblance to a good steak, in flavor if not in texture, is quite remarkable.

Drying Mushrooms *

Mushrooms may be preserved entire by drying them in the sun or in an oven. All moisture must be removed before the material is packed in a perfectly tight container. Mushrooms so preserved, after a preliminary soaking in tepid water or milk, may be cooked as if fresh.

Dried mushrooms, and even tough dried stems, may be ground and used as a powder for seasoning gravies and other dishes.

* From the U.S.D.A. Bull. No. 796.

Bibliography and Index

Bibliography

ATKINSON, GEORGE F. *Mushrooms*. Ithaca: Andrus and Church, 1901.

CLEMENTS, FREDERIC E. *Minnesota Mushrooms*. Minneapolis: University of Minnesota Plant Studies (No. IV). 1910.

COKER, W. C. *The Clavarias of the United States and Canada*. Chapel Hill: University of North Carolina Press. 1923.

—— "The Lactarias of North Carolina," *Journal of the Elisha Mitchell Scientific Society*, Vol. 34, Nos. 1 and 2 (June 1918).

COKER, W. C., and JOHN N. COUCH. *The Gastromycetes of the Eastern United States and Canada*. Chapel Hill: University of North Carolina Press. 1928.

COOKE, M. C. *British Edible Fungi*. London: Kegan Paul, Trench, Trübner and Co. 1891.

GÜSSOW, H. T., and W. S. ODELL. *Mushrooms and Toadstools*. Ottawa: Division of Botany, Dominion Experimental Farms. 1928.

HARD, M. E. *The Mushroom*. Columbus: Mushroom Publishing Co. 1908.

HAY, W. DELISLE. *The Fungus-Hunter's Guide*. London: Swan Sonnenschein, Lowry and Co. 1887.

KAUFFMAN, C. H. *Agaricaceae of Michigan*. 2 vols. Lansing: Michigan Geological and Biological Survey Publication No. 26 (Biol. Series 5). 1918.

KRIEGER, LOUIS, C. C. *A Popular Guide to the Higher Fungi (Mushrooms) of New York State*. New York State Museum Handbook No. 11. Albany: University of the State of New York. 1935.

McILVAINE, CHARLES, and ROBERT K. MACADAM. *One Thousand American Fungi*. Indianapolis: Bowen-Merrill Co. 1902.

PATTERSON, FLORA W., and VERA K. CHARLES. *Some Common Edible and Poisonous Mushrooms*. U. S. Department of Agriculture, Farmers' Bulletin No. 796. Washington: Government Printing Office. 1922.

RIPPERGER, HELMUT. *Mushroom Cookery*. New York: George W. Stewart. 1941.

ROLFE, R. T., and F. W. ROLFE. *The Romance of the Fungus World*. London: Chapman and Hall, Ltd. 1925.

STEP, EDWARD. *Toadstools and Mushrooms of the Countryside*. London: Hutchinson and Co. 1913.

SWANTON, E. W. *Fungi and How to Know Them*. London: Methuen and Co. 1909.

THOMAS, WILLIAM S. *Field Book of Common Gilled Mushrooms*. New York: G. P. Putnam's Sons. 1928.

MUSHROOM CULTIVATION

CHARLES, VERA K. *Mushroom Culture for Amateurs*. U. S. Department of Agriculture, Farmers' Bulletin No. 1587. Washington: Government Printing Office. 1929.

COMMON EDIBLE MUSHROOMS

DEFRIES, A. *The Book of the Mushroom*. London: Methuen and Co. 1936.

LAMBERT, EDMUND B. "Principles and Problems of Mushroom Culture," *Botanical Review*, 4:397–426 (1938).

MAHONEY, C. H., E. A. BESSEY, and E. I. McDANIEL. *Commercial Mushroom Production*. East Lansing: Michigan State College, Agricultural Experiment Station Bulletin No. 158. 1936.

RETTEW, G. RAYMOND, OTIS E. GAHM, and FLOYD W. DIVINE. *Manual of Mushroom Culture*. West Chester, Pennsylvania: Chester County Mushroom Laboratories. 1938.

Index

The various kinds of mushrooms are indexed by both scientific and common names, when they have common names. Numbers in italics refer to main headings; others refer to incidental mention or, more often, to figures.

E69631

6.95

Christensen, Clyde Martin, 1905–
  Common edible mushrooms, by Clyde M. Christensen ...
Minneapolis, The University of Minnesota press ₍1943₎

  x, 124 p. illus., 4 col. pl. (incl. front.) 21ᶜᵐ.
  Bibliography: p. 119–120.

1. Mushrooms—U. S. 2. Cookery (Mushrooms)   ɪ. Title.

43–52551

2/88